# THE CAPTAIN'S TABLE

# *The* CAPTAIN'S TABLE

*Life and dining on the great ocean liners*

SARAH EDINGTON

CONWAY

NATIONAL
MARITIME
MUSEUM

© National Maritime Museum, 2005 (unless otherwise indicated)

First published in 2005 by
National Maritime Museum Publishing,
Greenwich, London, SE10 9NF

This edition published in Great Britain in 2011 by Conway,
an imprint of Anova Books Ltd
10 Southcombe Street
London
W14 0RA

www.conwaypublishing.com
www.anovabooks.com
www.nmm.ac.uk

10 9 8 7 6 5 4 3 2 1

A CIP catalogue record of this book is available from the British
Library.

ISBN 9781844861453

Printed and bound by Toppan Leefung Printers Ltd, China.

Frontispiece: Louis XVI Dining Salon on the *Aquitania*, 1914, Cunard.

# Contents

◇

◇

P&O MENU

# *Acknowledgements*

*Menu, Moldavia,*
*1935, P&O.*

I would particularly like to thank: Sally and Jeremy Spooner, Helen Milner, Margaret Gale, Janet Date, Pen Gingell, Cecilia Hulse, Doug Day and Maureen Germany for sharing their experiences as passengers and crew on the liners with me; Pauline Dellar for introducing me to David Padmore; David Padmore himself, who brought to life the varied experiences of a chief purser on Union-Castle Line and who provided invaluable answers to my questions; Anthony Barnes for allowing me to quote from his parents' letters; John Graves for helping me with historical accuracy; Stephen Rabson, P&O Archivist, for his help; Mike Monahan, Executive Chef at P&O for information on today's menus; Malcolm Hillier for lending me cook books that were no longer in print; Kate Steggles who checked the recipes; Alison Moss for editing; and Fiona, my writer daughter, who read and commented on my prose.

Thanks also go to all the volunteers from the National Maritime Museum who valiantly cooked, ate, drank and reported on the recipes; Rachel Giles for giving me the chance to be involved with this project; Eli Dryden, Hellen Pethers and the staff of the library at the National Maritime Museum for all their help and patience in tracking down books for me.

And last but not least, John, who encouraged me, ate with enthusiasm, and without whom the manuscript would undoubtedly have been late.

I have enjoyed every minute of this book. As you will see the menus themselves are both fascinating and beautiful. It has been rewarding delving back to find the recipes, the stories behind them and the magnificent meals that were provided throughout the years on the great liners that sailed the oceans of the world. In the words of all the people I talked to who travelled, and worked on them, 'the food was superb'.

*Bon Appetit!*

# WELCOME ABOARD

*'Ships at a distance have every man's wish on board'*

Zora Neale Hurston

The dictionary definition of a voyage is 'a journey, especially by sea'. From the middle of the nineteenth century that journey was most probably made on a steamship or liner. People travelled for all kinds of reasons: for pleasure, for work, to start a new life or to escape from an impossible one. The voyages sometimes took weeks, at other times just days. First-Class passengers made that journey in the lap of luxury, steerage had to live cheek by jowl in the bowels of the ship, and those travelling Second Class were accommodated in modest cabins of two or four, sleeping in narrow bunks. Each class kept to its own part of the ship. Their experiences of shipboard life were very different but whatever their circumstances, they had to be fed.

*The Captain's Table* looks at life at sea through the dishes that were offered on the ships' menus. The earliest I looked at was the Bill of Fare on the Peninsular and Orient Steam Navigation (P&O) Company's *Pera* on 14 September 1859. The most modern was the Farewell Dinner on the last voyage of Union-Castle's *Windsor Castle* on 17 September 1977, just one night before Southampton and retirement. The most lavish menus were those of the great liners crossing the North Atlantic in the 1930s. This tradition continued into the 1960s and later. Of course, the chefs on the *Queen Mary*, *Queen Elizabeth* and *Normandie* had only five or six days in which to 'wow' their clientele. Union-Castle's ships took a fortnight to reach Capetown. P&O's Australian and Far Eastern routes had their passengers on board for even longer.

Many people talked to me about their experiences on the ships. Whether they had worked on them, travelled as passengers, or even done both, they unanimously agreed that the food was superb. So within these pages you will find almost seventy recipes that recreate the experience in those dining saloons where stewards, in the words of one proud captain, 'flitted like devoted acolytes'. Where the dishes have a particular history or tale to tell I have included it. I have taken care to choose recipes that are possible for the cook at home. The professional kitchen is a different place – a chef does not have to worry about charming his guests with his presence – so I avoided most recipes that needed a last minute flourish or split-second timing.

Besides satisfying appetites, mealtimes had another important function: they gave the long day at sea a structure, a timetable for living. The crew had their watches; the passengers had their meals. Perhaps this is the reason why they were so elaborate: there were four courses at

Farewells on the quayside, *Windsor Castle*, c.1960, Union-Castle.

breakfast, four again at lunchtime and often five at dinner. And these meals ate up time as well. Add into this timetable, beef tea in cold climes and fruit juice in the tropics at 11 a.m., afternoon tea at 4.30 p.m. and cocktails at 7 p.m. and you have filled much of your day. But of course, you need an appetite to do justice to it all, and life at sea is not just about food. So how was life at sea?

Of course, it changed over the years. In the nineteenth century, the ships were smaller and more at risk from the weather. Few people travelled for pleasure: the absence of stabilizers and seasickness pills meant that passage by sea was not particularly pleasant. Tables had fiddle boards, which were raised wooden rims, and in rough weather, stewards dampened the tablecloths before laying up to stop cutlery and crockery sliding. When the sea was calm and the sun shone, conversation with other passengers on deck in the day and cards and perhaps some impromptu music in the saloon in the evening were the norm. Time could pass very slowly. The novelist William Thackeray did travel round the

Dinner during rough weather on a P&O ship in the Bay of Biscay in the nineteenth century.

Mediterranean for pleasure in 1854. One of the ships was P&O's *Lady Mary Wood*. He wrote a highly entertaining account of his voyage acutely observing not only the ports they called at but also the crew: 'this knot of good fellows'. He enjoyed his voyage, but felt compelled at one point to write: 'In the week we were on board – it seemed a year, by the way'.

The years I am going to concentrate on are those of the first seven decades of the twentieth century. By 1912, steam had replaced sail everywhere. In the North Atlantic, the Cunard Line had the transatlantic mail contract. However, the profit lay in carrying passengers, and the huge numbers of emigrants packed into steerage was where the real money was made, with the rich in First Class providing the icing on the cake. Jews from Russia, Poland and Lithuania, Armenians from Turkey, the Irish poor, all converged on the northern ports of Europe hoping for a new life free from poverty and persecution in the USA. The larger the ship, the more she could carry and the safer she looked to the emigrants, who chose their ship, not like those in First Class for the service they had received or on the advice of friends, but according to the size and number of funnels. The *Mauretania*, *Olympic*, *Titanic*, *Aquitania* and *Lusitania* had four funnels. The *Atlantic*, *Imperator*, *France*, *Cordilliere*, amongst others, had three funnels but were just as large. They sailed back and forth between the Old and the New Worlds with their cargoes of souls. Nobody told the passengers that sometimes the final funnel was there just to impress and didn't actually function.

Everything started to change after the US Immigration Restriction Act in 1921, which instilled quotas for immigrants. Ships had to reorganize their classes and find new passengers and new routes in the off season for transatlantic travel. The pleasure cruise was born and with it the Tourist Class. By the end of the 1920s, ships such as the *Laconia* cruised in the Mediterranean and the Caribbean in the off season, with their quota of First Class but also a new type of passenger, the young or less well-off travelling for pleasure and adventure. Of course, there were shipping lines that had always taken passengers of all classes for long distances; P&O, serving India and the Far East, was already an institution. Union-Castle sailed regularly to Capetown. With the advent of oil power instead of coal, and more stable ships, the experience that had hitherto been an endurance test became one that you could enjoy.

## LIFE ABOARD

Early emigrants took their own food, but from the middle of the nineteenth century meals were included in the price of a ticket in steerage. There was no choice and the food was just about edible. Emigrants at that time slept in dormitories with no privacy and no stowage space; sometimes they had to bring their own bedding. Things improved in the first decade of the twentieth century as shipping companies started to care for their poorest passengers. Blankets and linen were provided and quantities of food became more generous. I found this notice on the bottom of a menu on an emigrant ship, the *Benalla*, taking passengers to Australia in 1915: 'It is the P&O Company's wish that passengers should have an ample supply of food. Anyone not receiving this should report the matter at once'.

Space was minimal. Steerage or Third-Class passengers sometimes found themselves sixteen to a dormitory. The *Titanic* charged more and was correspondingly much more comfortable but the Third-Class cabins were internal and deep in the ship: a smaller percentage of Third-Class passengers survived her sinking than in the other two classes.

Second-Class cabins were more spacious, although even after the Second World War you might still be called upon to share with a stranger. Women travelling alone were asked to share with other unaccompanied women, and men were roomed similarly. 'It was useful if you got on, because this called for a bit of arranging, of course, when you saw someone you fancied', remembers a young male passenger in the 1950s.

First-Class cabins were situated in the centre of the ship, which was the best place in terms of stability, and of course, had a porthole or portholes. In general, they were lavishly decorated. Suites often had two bedrooms, two bathrooms and a sitting room. On some ships servant accommodation was incorporated as part of the suite.

Class divisions were rigidly enforced. Everything happened separately. Eating, drinking, recreation, even the part of the deck for strolling, was segregated. You could visit the class above if invited and with permission from the chief steward, but fraternizing was frowned upon. In the 1950s, Helen Wilmerding, a young American, was travelling to Europe: 'I was travelling with a girl friend, Second Class, when we were students at university, I remember we saw our friends travelling First once by invitation. It wasn't encouraged'. Church Service on a Sunday morning was one of the few occasions when the classes

First-Class (top) and Third-Class (bottom) smoking rooms on the *Mauretania*, Cunard.

mixed and First Class were joined by the other classes. Sometimes the Second Class joined the First Class for frog racing or quiz games.

Third-Class passengers were thankful to be on their way to a new life. But how did the pampered rich occupy their time at sea?

## DRESS

Much time was spent changing clothes. Passengers travelled with huge amounts of luggage. Some of it was labelled 'Not Wanted on Voyage' and was stored in the hold, but there were probably still several cabin trunks. The best of these were fitted efficiently with drawers on the right and hanging space on the left. The Duke and Duchess of Windsor always had at least ninety pieces of luggage with them. Eventually Cunard told them gently that they could not handle so much and the Duke and Duchess changed line. Socialites ashore in the 1920s changed their clothes five times a day, and so it was at sea. From the first turn round the deck after breakfast to the last dance of the evening, every event and every meal could justify a new outfit. Several of the liners had staircases that seem designed entirely for grand entrances. Gentlemen needed informal clothes for the day, sports clothes when required and formal dinner jackets or tails for the evening. It was all highly time-consuming. Fine laundering was provided, accommodation for servants next door to the best suites was *de rigueur*, and of course there were beauty salons and barbershops helping to keep sir and madam looking their best.

The Duke and Duchess of Windsor on board the *Queen Mary*, c. 1920, Cunard.

## DÉCOR

Those travelling First Class demanded the best and, as a result, ships were equipped with gymnasiums, swimming pools, Turkish baths and jacuzzis, squash and racquets courts, tennis courts, smoking rooms, libraries, cinemas, card rooms, ladies' drawing rooms and ballrooms complete with piano – bolted to the floor of course. Sometimes they had casinos. And of course, they had dining saloons of spectacular size and elegance.

The sleek lines of the ship overall, dedicated as she was to carving her way through the waves as speedily as possible, gave way inside to a fantasy world, fortunately captured for us in photographs. It was as if the more the décor was rooted in the land, the better it could control the dangerous, unsettling presence of the sea. First Class seemed to prefer a style that was a throwback to a past age when the aristocracy thrived. It was an anti-industrial look despite the up-to-date machinery driving the ship.

The huge ships built between 1890 and the Second World War were decorated in the most exuberant, elaborate styles. The public spaces were vast, the styles eclectic. There were ships with Egyptian, Italian Renaissance, Moorish, Spanish, Louis XIV, Empire, Georgian, Queen Anne, Jacobean and Tudor interiors. And no one style prevailed throughout: some ships incorporated several of these different styles simultaneously. What they shared was a love of grandeur; panelling, pillars, marble fireplaces, carving, and murals were used in abundance. Carpets were deep-pile; curtains were damask or velvet. Furniture was often French style, with gilded frames and tapestry seats. Potted palms and huge arrangements of flowers occupied every available space.

The Honourable Elsie Mackay, daughter of the chairman of P&O, was given responsibility for the interior décor for the Company's ships built in the 1920s. Splendid up-to-date equipment was installed, such as electric lifts, electric radiators and forced air ventilation instead of fans. Elsie's décor, however, harked back to the pre-industrial world. Her last commission was the *Viceroy of India*, which came into commission in 1929. The First-Class smoking room was oak panelled, with a huge fireplace that had a royal coat of arms as an overmantel, leaded windows with stained glass escutcheons and wrought iron gates. The atmosphere was that of a Tudor palace or Scottish baronial hall. Elsie was influenced by accounts of James I's palace at Bromley-by-Bow. By contrast the music room and the dining room were eighteenth century

and the swimming pool had classical pillars and reliefs in the style of the lost city of Pompeii.

A new style of décor arrived in 1925 with the Compagnie Générale Transatlantique's (CGT) elegant *Ile de France*. She was excitingly modern. Thirty of Europe's top designers were involved in fitting her out in the Art Deco style. All about movement, it was a style that seemed made for the new liners. She reigned as the ship of choice for the young chic traveller, including the stars of the newly expanding world of the movies, until two ships that were to dominate the North Atlantic until the Second World War arrived on the scene.

They were the French *Normandie*, reckoned by some to be the most beautiful ship ever built, and the British *Queen Mary*. At the time, at 79,000 and 80,773 tons respectively, they were the largest and the fastest ships afloat. Great rivals, they were commissioned within a year of each other and competed fiercely for passengers. The *Normandie* was superbly decorated; the most famous room – the First-Class salle à manger, or dining saloon – was 282 feet long and three decks high. Twenty-foot bronze doors opened on to a room decorated with onyx, gold and crystal. It was lined with illuminated glass fountains designed by Lalique and at one end there was a *grande descente*, a huge staircase just made for spectacular entries. No wonder movie stars such as Marlene Dietrich travelled in her.

Cunard's *Queen Mary* carried the prestige of Britain on her elegant decks. Her décor, too, was Art Deco, but whereas the *Normandie* was compared to a palace, the *Queen Mary* has been compared to a grand country house. And what brought passengers back again and again to the *Queen Mary* was the quality and care of the service.

Opposite: First-Class smoking room on the *Viceroy of India*, 1929, P&O.

Right: Menu (detail), *Pendennis Castle*, 1959, Union-Castle.

## CAPTAIN AND CREW

It was not the beauty of the ship, her speed, the nationality of the line owning her, nor even the food which made people fiercely loyal to one particular line or ship, it was the crew.

In overall charge was the captain. On a master's ticket, the qualification that entitles the holder to command a ship, it describes him as 'master before God'. He wielded absolute power in this 'world within a world'; in the nineteenth century, his remit even extended to ensuring punctuality at mealtimes. A young banker travelling to Hong Kong comments: 'Lunch was at 1 p.m., dinner at 7 p.m. If you were late…

Meeting the captain,
*Orsova*, 1955, P&O.

you had to start your lunch at whatever course the Captain was eating'. He was, of course, the holder of a master's ticket with years of experience at sea behind him, responsible for conducting the huge ship with its complement of passengers and crew through whatever weather they might encounter. He had to command the respect of the crew, who were often from very different backgrounds. He also had to charm or at least manage the passengers.

Cunard White Star was very proud of its captains who were called commodores. This commendation dates to the late 1930s: 'All of our twenty-four captains are officers in the Royal Navy Reserve. Twenty-two have the Royal Decorations. Six are Officers of the Order of the British Empire. Two have the Distinguished Service Cross. One is a Baronet. One is Aide de Camp to His Majesty King Edward VIII…an honour, the highest that can be conferred, granted to one only in the merchant service'.

P&O officers were also often members of the Royal Navy Reserve and their captains were known always as commanders. Amongst the crew they were generally known as 'the old man'. Their commodore was the senior captain of the whole line. Their ships were run along navy lines. However, the liner captains had a further responsibility as part of the trip, as Commander Gordon Steele VC RN comments: 'Every Captain of a liner is supposed to be a "character" otherwise he would not attract passengers to his ship. It does not matter what form his peculiarity takes. I have known rude Captains, polite Captains, Captains who are fond of children, Captains who are fond of the ladies and Captains who are fond of neither. I have sailed with liberal drinking Captains and with teetotal Captains'.

Apart from the captain, responsibilities on ships were divided into three departments – the deck officers, the engine room and the purser's department. Next down in line was the chief officer. He was the sea-borne equivalent of the chief executive and was responsible jointly with the captain for safe navigation. The second officer looked after cargo, cleanliness and the navigation instruments. The third officer was responsible for the mail. This was a very important role; many of the ships discussed here had a contract with their respective governments to carry the mail. The fourth officer took charge of baggage and the fifth officer for the bullion room. These deck and navigation officers were responsible for manoeuvring, including steering and docking, and navigation. Under their control were the deck hands who might do any job relating to the maintenance of the ship, act as lookouts and helmsmen on the bridge, help with mooring up, fire and security, and taking on stores.

The engineering department was headed up by the chief engineering officer, assisted by at least three other engineer officers, an electrical officer and a radio officer. The ship's engineers had complete responsibility for the ship's engine room and the electrical generation plant. It was a 'hands on' job, hard physical work for all, including the officers. Traditionally, many chief engineers were Scottish, swapping the chill of their homeland for cramped hot engine rooms. 'Our chief engineer was a crusty old Scot but he melted after a drink into being quite friendly with us girls', says Margaret Gale, who was working her passage to Australia as a children's hostess in 1960. Early chief engineers needed to be tough. They controlled the stokers. Until the change from coal to oil as fuel the stokers or 'black gang' were a breed apart. Deep in the bowels of the ship, black from coal dust, they tended to be illiterate, desperately poor men. Theirs was a dangerous, exhausting job in terrible conditions. When the captain rang down for speed, the chief engineer set a number. If it was seven, the gang had seven minutes to cut the soft coal, rake out the grates, and shovel in a new load before the bell rang. Then the operation was repeated again and again. The heat was intense, so the men worked bare-chested, wearing thick gloves and wooden clogs. Add to the heat the rolling motion of the ship, the incessant din of the engines, the ever-present red-hot coals, and the boiler room must have been a kind of living hell. Oil made life more bearable in the boiler rooms but the 'black gang' were now unemployed.

The deck and engineering crews had always been made up of many nationalities and formed tight-knit communities within the ship. For instance, P&O, serving the British Empire in the east, traditionally recruited crews from India. These particular crew members were known as 'Lascars'. Different parts of India supplied different elements of the crew. Deck crews, known as 'Kalasis', and engine room crew mostly came from Muslim India or Pakistan. In their charge was a 'Serang' who might have many years of service behind him as well as many other members of his extended family on the ships. Sarfaraz Khan, chief engine room Serang on the liner *Arcadia*, served P&O for thirty-six years and had seventeen members of his family also working on the ships.

Another group of Lascars were Christian Indians from Goa. Their religion permitted them to handle all meat and fish, unlike their Muslim and Hindu compatriots, so they were ideal recruits for the third department of the ship, the steward's department, which, for this book, is probably the most important since food and service were under its control. In overall charge in this department was the chief steward or purser. He organized the ordering of stores or 'victualling', a huge logistical task on any ship.

The ship's band play on a Spanish night, *Oronsay*, c. 1925.

# VICTUALLING

Here is a list of some of the staples required for a single voyage on the
*Queen Mary* across the Atlantic from Southampton to New York. This
would have fed 2000 passengers and nearly 1000 crew.

20 tons of beef
25 tons of potatoes
4000 lb of tea and coffee
70,000 eggs
1000 jars of jam
5 tons of bacon and ham
160 gallons of salad oil
9 tons of fish
½ ton of bananas
500 lb of smoked salmon
4½ tons of lamb

In the nineteenth century some meat had to be salted, although ships
did have cold rooms packed with ice. Twentieth-century refrigeration
brought greater choice. P&O owned farms along their routes, allowing
fresh fruit and vegetables to be loaded aboard at ports of call.

The bar on the *Queen Mary* carried for the same trip:

5000 bottles of spirits
40,000 bottles of beer
10,000 bottles of table wine
60,000 bottles of mineral water
6000 gallons of draught ale
5000 cigars
20,000 packets of cigarettes

These quantities are given for a voyage in the 1930s. Prohibition,
restricting the sale of alcohol in the USA, was an incentive for going to
sea in the 1920s. Add to that the fact that shipboard drink was duty-free
in international waters and it is not surprising that shipping lines found
short 'booze cruises' from port to port in America and Australia a useful
source of income.

## THE PURSER

The purser hired the chefs, the cooks, the kitchen porters and those who washed the dishes. He also controlled the stewards and stewardesses, the swimming pool attendants, the barmen, the beauticians, the bellboys, the barber and the band amongst others. Apart from the odd glimpse of the captain and the deck crew, these were the people with whom the passengers would have contact and whose demeanour would make or break the passage or holiday for them.

A seasoned passenger always made contact with the purser as soon as possible, as it was he who assigned cabins, organized entertainment, supervised the arrival and departure of passengers, stored their jewellery, listened to complaints, and played 'host'. Most important, he controlled the seating arrangements in the dining saloon and steamer chairs on deck. Ambitious social climbers would try and bribe stewards to be placed near the latest celebrity. American mothers would hope to see their daughter placed near money, an English lord or Italian prince; businessmen took the opportunity to pursue a possible financier. A good purser presided over a 'happy ship', quite an achievement with sometimes difficult people.

## MORNINGS

Days at sea began early for the crew. Margaret Gale remembers: 'I always had to be up by 6.30 even on Christmas Day, however late we had been to bed'. Reveille was not so early for the passengers. Breakfast could be taken in the saloon, but many First-Class passengers preferred the luxury of breakfast in bed brought by their steward or stewardess. Every ship printed a daily newspaper, which would arrive with breakfast. As there were no telephones in the cabins until the 1930s, this was the only way of knowing what was going on in the outside world. It usually included some international news and a timetable for that day that detailed all the activities on offer. *The Normandie*'s newspaper was called *L'Atlantique*, the *Himalaya*'s was the *Himalaya Observer*, and the *Queen Mary* had the *Atlantic Chronicle*.

## SPORTS

Mornings were spent, for the lazy, tucked up in a steamer chair reading the latest novel; for the energetic, walking on deck or playing the various sports available.

Keep fit class,
Union-Castle.

Some sports were particular to shipboard life. Deck quoits of all kinds, played with rings made of rope, was invented in the nineteenth century and is still played on ships today. Shuffleboard was played with a kind of puck on the end of a long stick. Helen Wilmerding remembers it 'like a giant version of Shove Ha'penny'. Quoits and Shuffleboard tournaments were organized and were always very competitive. In the 1950s, Helen's sister Jan 'got up specially early. She liked to win and often did'. Many ships ran keep-fit or yoga classes. Shaw, Savill and Albion Line's *Andes* cruising south in the 1960s offered 'Slim and Trim with Janet on the Sun Deck'. Janet doubled as dancer in the evening shows and as a ballroom instructor with her dance partner in the afternoons.

Earlier in the century, the roll call of sports on the smaller ships making the long journey east comes across rather like a children's primary school sports day. Egg-and-spoon races, sack races, potato races, threadneedle races and tugs of war all get a mention. Did gentleman participate in the skipping contests? Contestants competed as a couple in the tie and cigarette race, the bottle race and the whistle and biscuit race. The men's games, such as slinging the monkey, spar fighting and 'chalk the mark' – described as 'hanging by the ankles and heels, etc.' – sound rather more dangerous. Even on these ships, deck cricket matches were played between teams from the first and second saloon, for instance, and between ladies and gentlemen. In the latter scenario the gentlemen had to bat and bowl left handed and the account comments on the number of balls that were lost overboard. Pillow fighting on a pole over the pool was initially enjoyed by the gentlemen but became popular with the ladies as well.

By the 1930s, most of the children's games had disappeared. The ships were getting much larger: the only pre-Second World War ship to have a full-size tennis court was the *Normandie* but deck tennis, a scaled down version of the land game, was played as were badminton and table tennis. The large liners had squash, racquet courts and gymnasiums. The equipment was rather different. There is an apocryphal tale that an archbishop fell off a mechanical camel on a Cunard ship crossing the Atlantic in the 1920s. There are photographs of fencing and boxing matches. Tug of war contests survive from the earlier days as does deck cricket.

Above: Deck Quoits on the *Strathmore*, 1938, P&O.

Opposite: Games in the pool, *Empress of Canada*, 1961, Canadian Pacific.

'The ship is like a palace. There is an uninterrupted deck run of 165 yards for our use, and a ripping swimming bath'. This is Hugh Woolner, a First-Class passenger writing about the ill-fated *Titanic* before she sank after a collision with an iceberg on her maiden voyage. In 1912 White Star's elegant ship was the largest in the world. By the 1930s, if strolling

The swimming pool,
*Oronsay, c.* 1951,
Orient Line.

and swimming were your preferred form of exercise, all the ships had
spacious decks large enough both for the loungers and the speed walkers.
Most of the ships by this time had interior swimming pools, often with
exotic décor. No less than four ships, the *Viceroy of India, Georgic,
Saturnia* and *Vulcania* had pools with a Pompeian theme. Ancient Egypt
was the inspiration for the *Queen Mary's* indoor pool.

## CARDS AND GAMBLING

Not everyone was taking exercise or enjoying the sea breezes. Gambling
was a part of shipboard life. All the liners had card rooms. Fortunes
were made and lost during the voyage. Bridge friends booked holidays
together and didn't allow landfall to interrupt the game. 'I remember
when we arrived at Rio de Janeiro which was spectacular; there were
bridge players who never left the card room while we were in port.

They came on a cruise to play bridge with their friends and they were going to play, whatever the distractions', recalled one passenger. Cardsharps were a permanent hazard. What did you do if you were the captain and it had been brought to your attention that someone, who had a history of sharp dealing, was on the ship? A friendly chat in the captain's cabin with his large pistol on the desk was one captain's method. Nothing could be done, however, until a crime was committed. On board ship passengers gambled on everything.

Every ship ran a daily tote with the aim to guess the number of miles covered each day, the more technical participants allowing for fluctuations in speed due to inclement weather conditions. Inside knowledge helped: indeed regular travellers became adept at guessing correctly. The same competitor frequently won the coveted daily prize. It was yet another reason for loyalty to the same ship.

## THE BLUE RIBAND

For some ships the daily run became a matter of national pride. The Blue Riband was a notional trophy for the fastest crossing by a liner between England's Bishop Rock and New York's Ambrose Light. It preoccupied every line steaming between Europe and America. The amount of coal consumed to enable the ship to steam at full speed might be double the normal consumption so it was enormously expensive. And yet it caught the imagination of everyone. The companies saw enormous prestige in it; the country of the ship that held it basked in reflected glory and the passengers on that particular crossing would see it as a high point in their lives.

During the trip, as passengers studied the daily run, news of the attempt would leak out, excitement would mount, and huge sums would be staked for or against the ship achieving it. In July 1929 when Germany's *Bremen* took the Blue Riband from Britain's *Mauretania* after twenty-two years, she was met by cheering crowds and a band when she reached New York. France's *Normandie* also gained the coveted prize on her maiden voyage in 1935. She achieved it by maintaining an average speed of 30.5 knots per hour and her time was 4 days, 3 hours and 2 minutes which clipped 14 hours and 58 minutes off the *Bremen*'s time. Excited passengers and crew were so certain of victory that they started wearing blue the night before. A huge banner of blue muslin 98 feet long was flown as she reached New York.

When the *Queen Mary* was commissioned in 1936, the Blue Riband shuttled back and forth between the two ships for a year or two. In August 1938 the *Queen Mary* won it at a speed of 31.69 knots. Britain and France went to war against Germany in September 1939 and so the *Queen Mary* held the record until 1952 when the brand new American *United States* gained the coveted prize. The voyage took an astonishing 3 days, 10 hours and 40 minutes. The ship steamed so fast she stripped the paint from her waterline: her speed was faster than 35 knots but the actual figures are a military secret as she was designed to become a top speed troopship in wartime. She is retired now, but she still holds the westbound Blue Riband.

## THE SECOND WORLD WAR

Most passenger ships in commission in 1939 were taken over by their respective navies during the Second World War except the beautiful *Normandie* disastrous fire destroyed her in her berth at Pier 90 in New York before the refit for trooping was finished. Alongside her in 1940 were the other two super liners of the Atlantic, her rival the *Queen Mary* and the *Mary*'s younger sister, the even larger *Queen Elizabeth*. The *Queen Elizabeth*'s first years were spent as a troopship with the *Queen Mary* ferrying huge numbers of troops, first to the Far East when the Japanese and Americans entered the war and later zigzagging across the Atlantic (to dodge the U-boats) in preparation for the D-Day invasion of Europe. During this period the elegant staterooms for two held forty soldiers on a hot bunk system of two shifts a night. Two meals a day were served to the men and stewards found their

VE Day Dinner Menu, *Circassia*, 8 May 1945, Anchor Line.

Menu
"VE" DAY DINNER

Cream A la Truman

Steak and Kidney Pie, Montgomery
Garden Peas, Portal
Potatoes El Alemien

Admiral Cunningham Pudding

Alexander Victory Fruit

Coffee Merchant Navy

V

H.M.Transport "CIRCASSIA"
Tonnage 11,135 Tons. Gross.

The Circassia is an Anchor Line ship.Her port of Registry is Glasgow. Her people-the Master,Officers,and Men-are manned by the Company in Glasgow and throughout all her employment she has been maintained from the Clyde.In 1939 she was fitted as an Armed Merchant Cruiser and sailed in enforcement of our cause as H.M.S. "Circassia". In 1942 she was converted to be a Troopship. As a Troopship she has carried over 71,000 Officers and Men.She was present,as a first line assault ship,In the landings at Sicily, Nettuno,and South of France,and was always able to do whatever was required of her.

The Circassia salutes you all on this Great Day.
8. 5. 1945.

duties were rather different than in peacetime. A P&O steward relates: 'As there were 7000 men to receive five slices of bread each day, this meant around 35,000 slices.... The bread was cut into slices by two men who also chopped up 56 pound boxes of frozen butter. They then melted it to a liquid in the galley oven. The remainder of us were lined up behind a bench, which had a marble top, where we applied the butter to the bread with 2-inch paintbrushes. Of course a lot of the loose hairs from the brushes ended up on the bread'.

The *Queen Mary*'s last job as a troopship was taking 1100 GI brides with their 900 babies to the USA. At long last she could return to her role as a passenger liner. The *Queen Elizabeth* finally made her maiden voyage with paying passengers on 25 July 1947.

The next ten years were the golden years for the liners. They ruled the North Atlantic run until the advent of airliners signalled the end of an era. This was the way to cross 'the pond'. Great care was taken that the passengers on the *Queen Mary* and *Queen Elizabeth* would see the other when they crossed in mid-Atlantic. Union-Castle ships also waved at each other off the coast of West Africa on the run between Southampton and Capetown. Of course, the exact time these events would happen was yet another opportunity for a bet.

When they were not carrying Americans to Europe and vice versa, they took those who could afford it on cruises all over the world. Newly built ships or ships refitted after the war joined them. Union-Castle's elegant ships sailed 'every Thursday at 4 o'clock, to and from Capetown'. P&O and Orient Lines served the routes to and from Australia and the East.

## MENUS

The Luncheon Menus from these years are almost as lavish as the Dinner Menus. Reflecting the social realities outside this charmed world, as countries recovered from the privations of the Second World War, so the menus grew in size. By the beginning of the 1960s, they are very grand indeed with the whole menu printed in French on the left and translated into English on the right. If you could not find anything among the nineteen fish and meat dishes, the five puddings and the eleven cheeses offered, the chef had the solution. This challenge was printed on the Luncheon Menu from *Saxonia* on Monday, 28 August 1961: 'The Chef invites you to give him an opportunity to prepare your own favourite dish, whether it be a speciality of American, European or

Eastern Cuisine. He merely asks that you give the headwaiter sufficient notice in order for it to be prepared to perfection'.

## Emigrants to Australia

As well as the full-paying customers, a new generation of emigrants filled the ships heading east during the 1950s and 1960s. Under a shared British and Australian scheme, £10-per-head fares were offered to Britons with skills and their families prepared to work 'down under'. These emigrants were treated very differently from steerage. Good food, entertainment for the adults and schooling for the children were offered. It was an incredible opportunity to make a new life. You might not know your final destination, though. Margaret Gale, the children's hostess on the *Strathaird* on passage to Australia in 1960 remembers: 'In corners of the ship you could see people in earnest conversation usually with forms and a clipboard. These were Australian Immigration officials. They would interview emigrants, ask them their skill and then arrange for them to leave the ship at the port where there was work nearby. So people did not know whether they were going to Perth, Melbourne, Adelaide or Sydney. It depended on whether you were a plumber, an electrician or a stone mason'.

Margaret entertained and taught children in the mornings and afternoons but still found time to enjoy herself: 'The galley crew were mainly Goanese. So lunch was cold salads and always a different curry. We loved the curry. We had two hours off in the middle of the day. We used to rush up to the dining saloon, have our curry, a half hour for lunch and $1^1/_2$ hour's sleep. We needed that because our socializing started after we finished in the evening. Drinks in someone's cabin and we were up late. We met everybody'.

Follow my leader, *Windsor Castle*, c. 1960, Union-Castle.

## CELEBRITIES

After lunch, those of an active disposition could walk or play off their lunch; the indolent could tuck themselves back in their steamer chairs until teatime, from where they could play the universal game on ships of 'spot the celebrity'. The Passenger List, slipped under their door on the first night, would tell them who was on board. On occasion, they may have chosen their trip in the knowledge that they might catch a glimpse of a favourite actor or actress or even royalty.

Edward, Prince of Wales (later King Edward VIII), first crossed the Atlantic on the *Berengaria* in August 1924. The *Berengaria* had been Germany's flagship, the *Imperator*. Following the war it had been leased to Cunard as a British Government reparation and renamed. The Prince disguised himself by booking under the name of Lord Renfrew but of course it fooled no one. The ship was booked solid by Americans. Cunard ordered a band to meet him and swords to be worn, which threw the ship's officers into confusion. Luckily the Prince scotched all this. He wanted no special treatment and slipped on board, dodging the photographers from a launch in the Solent on the opposite side of the ship from the shore. Once on board, he enjoyed himself. He stayed in the Imperial Suite only ever previously occupied by the Kaiser. He did all the right things: attended Divine Service, led the tug of war (his side lost), was knocked off his pole in the pillow fight and lost his potato in the potato race. Every evening he indulged one of his greatest pleasures. He danced and danced, mostly with the ladies in his party, but occasionally some lucky American girl found herself swept off her feet and on to the dance floor to have something to talk about for the rest of her life.

Later, as the Duke of Windsor after he had abdicated from the throne, he and his American wife Wallis travelled with Cunard for many years. The crew on the *Queen Mary* remember them pacing the 'measured mile' round the deck each day, exercising their pug. Wallis is remembered as being a bit high-handed with the Duke from time to time and he would often visit the bridge late at night to chat with the officers and smoke his pipe. Perhaps it was also for a bit of peace.

Queen Elizabeth (later known as The Queen Mother), both with her husband George VI and on her own after his death, crossed many times on her namesake the *Queen Elizabeth*, and also on the *Queen Mary*. The

Marlene Dietrich – and her luggage – aboard the *Normandie*, 1938.

best time to spot her was at dinner. She had breakfast and lunch in her suite but ate in the Verandah Grill in the evening.

Many of the other royals on the passenger lists came from countries in which royalty is now a distant memory. Queen Marie of Romania was photographed arriving in New York. 'Look this way Queenie', shouted the photographers, and she did. King Zog of Albania travelled with his three beautiful sisters, known as 'the Zoglets'. The Shah of Persia crossed with his second wife, Queen Soraya. She is particularly remembered for her magnificent clothes. She changed several times a day and never repeated an outfit.

The film star who seems to have been photographed more than all the others throughout the heyday of the liners is Marlene Dietrich. The epitome of glamour, sometimes draped in furs, she posed leaning elegantly against the guardrail or surrounded by her luggage. She was never seen at breakfast, only occasionally at lunch, and timed her entrances for dinner to maximum effect. She shared her choice of dinner table on the *Queen Mary* with Noel Coward, the playwright and performer. Naturally, it was the most prominent in the dining saloon, but since they never travelled at the same time, this arrangement was perfect for both of them.

Coward first crossed the Atlantic in 1921 aged 22. He had conquered London and was confident that Broadway would welcome him too. He bought a one-way ticket on the *Aquitania*. After paying for his ticket and a suitcase for his new wardrobe he had less than £50 left and had to sell some songs in London to fund his trip.

All the celebrities had their favourite ship. Artist Salvador Dali and his glamorous wife Gala, film star James Stewart, the novelist Colette and the chanteuse Josephine Baker favoured the *Normandie*. Gloria Swanson, star of silent films, violinist Yehudi Menuhin and the conductor Arturo Toscanini preferred the *Ile de France*. Jazz greats Ella Fitzgerald and Duke Ellington, singer Bing Crosby and film star Cary Grant sailed on the *Queen Mary*. Grant called her 'the Eighth Wonder of the World'.

DIVING IS DANGEROUS

Crossing the Line
ceremony with King
Neptune and a subject,
*Windsor Castle, c. 1960,*
Union-Castle.

# CROSSING THE LINE

On the longer trips to and from the east, Australia, Cape Town and
South America, there was at least one afternoon or evening when a
peaceful doze was not a possibility. This was the day the ship crossed
the equator. Crossing the Line ceremonies were obligatory for anyone
crossing the equator for the first time. This seems to have been an excuse
for anarchy to break out. As Margaret Gale describes: 'The crew dressed
up as King Neptune and various fishy creatures'. In great maritime

tradition, Neptune and his court are solemnly received by the captain who then asks permission for the ship to cross the equator. Neptune grants the request on condition that 'all who have not crossed before must do homage to the king and be thrown overboard as a sacrifice to the fishes'. Then, as a gesture of goodwill, Neptune commutes the sentence to a dunking in the swimming pool. Men's faces are lathered with soot and shaved with a large wooden razor. Ladies faces are powdered with flour by the manicurist. There are a lot of soap suds involved; each person is pushed backward into the pool where sometimes mermaids, sometimes sea bears, duck them three times. It is good, boisterous fun and you do get a certificate, which you can display next time and avoid having to suffer again. There are also celebrations and a certificate on crossing the International Date Line in the Pacific and finding that you have lost or gained a complete day.

## PARTIES

Afternoon tea was the next event of the day. On the *Queen Mary* it was always at 4 p.m. exactly. Then it was time to change for dinner and the evening's entertainment. Before dinner though, there might be a party to go to.

Parties were part of the razzmatazz on every ship. As you unpacked you would look through the Passenger List to see if there were friends to meet up with or celebrities to look out for. If you decided to give your own party, invitations would be printed. You needed to make friends with the purser to be sure of the best arrangements. Probably the best course of all was to invite him to the party.

On every ship there was the Captain's Cocktail Party to look forward to. On the *Andes* it was held on the second night out. One of the entertainers remembers: 'Everyone wore their best, but if we were leaving Australia, the ladies would be togged up to the nines, while their menfolk would be making a point in shorts, vest and

Auld Lang Syne Farewell Dinner, *Lancastria*, 1935, Cunard.

thongs'. The *Andes* was a one-class ship, so the captain shook hands with every passenger. 'Everyone had an invitation so that meant 400 hands, if all the passengers attended'.

Everyone dressed up for the Captain's Cocktail Party on the *Orsova* in 1955. This meant dinner jackets for the men and cocktail dresses for the ladies. Sally Spooner's childhood memory brings the event vividly to life: 'We had an invitation to the Captain's Cocktail Party. We all dressed up. Sue and I wore dresses we had worn as bridesmaids earlier in the year. Mummy wore a cocktail dress and Daddy his dinner jacket. At the door everyone lined up to shake hands with the Captain. Mummy looked gorgeous and she was quite tall, the Captain was a small man. As she advanced towards him, he noted her with appreciation and planted his legs a little wider as if on deck in a rough sea before grasping her hand and welcoming her'.

## Dinner

Dinner followed. The most coveted invitation of all was to dine at the Captain's Table, although he might not be there too often in person. A girl who crossed the Atlantic in the 1950s remembers: 'My parents were always on the Captain's Table but I mostly remember him sending his excuses, saying that he was needed on the bridge or something'. Another intriguing question was who would dine on the Captain's Table with you. Sir George Barnes was Principal of Keele University crossing the Atlantic in 1956 on CGT's *Flandre*: 'I will keep this [letter] open until we have dined with the Captain to meet the Morgenthaus – Mrs. being a supreme eccentric who wears a yellow wig, prismatic glasses and is totally un-American in manner. … As well as the Morgenthaus, there was a Belgian aristocrat, and a Mme. de Caramon, lovely and intellectual, the French consul at Quebec, a Hungarian bag manufacturer and Mme. Auberton, the head of Solvay'.

Sir George listed the dinner menu. 'Dinner with the Captain (a thin intellectual from Nice) was one of the biggest ever meals with four choice wines, all French. Foie gras, turtle soup, sole, asparagus, tournedos, ices and fruit'. No wonder Lady Barnes had already written home that 'every meal is a delight'.

Sometimes meals were themed. St Patrick's Night in March or St Andrew's Night in November were wonderful excuses for the dishes to be suitably Irish or Scottish and to be written up in dialect which was

so broad as to be almost impenetrable. 'A Hunk o' Coo frae the Hielans'
is a good example. The *Circassia* was an Anchor Line ship fitted out
during the Second World War as an armed merchant cruiser. She
celebrated VE Day on 8 May 1945 with a dinner where every dish was
credited to the war. 'Cream a la Truman' was followed by 'Steak and
Kidney Pie Montgomery'. There was always a Bon Voyage, a Welcome
or a Get Together Dinner. Generally it took place on the second night
out. The first night was set aside for unpacking, familiarizing yourself
with the ship if it was your first trip and reacquainting yourself with
your favourite places and crew members if you had travelled in the ship
before. Likewise, there was always a Farewell Dinner, a Diner D'Adieu
or a Landfall Dinner at the end of the trip.

## ENTERTAINMENT

I was pleased to come across a Spanish Fiesta Night on a menu from the
*Queen Mary* in November in 1966. It gave me a chance to include one
of my favourite summer soups, Gazpacho. She was on a Mediterranean
cruise at the time. It is not clear on the menu, but my guess is that she
was moored in Malaga or Barcelona that night, and that flamenco
dancing by a local group would have been part of the entertainment
after dinner.

   I wonder if some enthusiastic flamenco lovers forwent their pudding
to get a good seat for the show. Evening entertainment was a huge part
of shipboard life. Before the First World War the entertainment was
generally home grown: passengers with a talent would gather in the
music room. Miss Holmes, travelling with P&O to India at the end of
the nineteenth century writes: 'A concert had been arranged for the final
evening in the music room and it was a very good performance, two
violin solos by Lady Mackenzie, several songs by Captain Caldbeck
(who is very clever, both in music and recitation) and some songs
exquisitely sung by the clergyman from the Second Saloon'.

   This tradition continued into the 1920s and 1930s. Artur Rubinstein,
the pianist, and Jascha Heifetz, the violinist, travelled as passengers on
the *Ile de France* and played on board. There is a tale that the captain
once poured oil on rough seas so that the great ballerina, Anna Pavlova,
could dance her 'Dying Swan' safely in mid-Atlantic.

   When professional musicians were first hired to play on the ships,
they had to double up as stewards, and this was not always very

Diner D'Adieu, *Australis*,
1932, Royal Mail Lines.

DINER D'ADIEU

41

successful. But post-Second World War it all became much more professional. Every ship had at least one band. 'On the *Andes*, we had a show band, a jazz quartet and two pianists', says Janet Date, who worked on the *Andes* as a dancer. 'We were some of the first to do proper shows, shortened versions of musicals like *No No Nanette* and *South Pacific*'.

   The great organizer of bands on the ships was Geraldo, born Gerald Bright in London in 1904. He had a famous residency at the Savoy Hotel in London and after the Second World War organized the dance bands on Cunard's liners. There was no shortage of young players signing up. The draw was not the pay, the sea air, the food or playing dance music on a pitching ship. It was the possibility of getting to see jazz heroes such as Charlie Parker or Dizzy Gillespie playing in New York. It's an odd

*No No Nanette* dancers, *Andes*, c. 1970s, Royal Mail Lines.

thought that the modern jazz scene in London evolved because young musicians such as Ronnie Scott and John Dankworth, who would never have been able to afford the fare, could play their way across the Atlantic. The most famous band of all is that on the *Titanic*, whose members were still playing when the ship went down. They were all lost and have become heroes of that dreadful night.

But bands and dancing have never been the only entertainment on board ship. Quizzes, films, tombola and guessing competitions vied with conjurors, comedians and lectures. Model frog, dog and horse racing were all popular, especially as they gave gamblers yet another chance to place a bet. Bingo, or 'Housie Housie' as it used to be called, was always a favourite.

Fancy Dress nights have always been part of shipboard life. On the *Orsova*, Sally Spooner and her twin improvised, but some people had come prepared. 'We had a fancy dress night on the *Orsova*. We were both gypsies, I was a boy and Sue was a gypsy girl in bare feet and hated it. Someone took a photo of us which she hated even more and in the background are two men dressed as Marilyn Monroe and Diana Dors, both massive. They must have brought the wigs with them specially for the occasion and you should have seen their huge red lipsticked mouths. They both look as though they are loving every minute'.

A show could be used to theme dinner, fancy dress, cabaret and help the local economy. 'We played *South Pacific* in the South Pacific. We also had a Fancy Dress Night where dinner featured fish and coconut of course, the cabaret had hula numbers and everyone wore grass skirts which they had bought at the last port of call'.

Fancy Dress Night,
*Orsova*, 1955, P&O.

## WEATHER

There was never a chance to be bored, although sometimes the weather took a hand. An Atlantic low could unmake the best arrangements. Cecilia Hulse, travelling between Britain and Canada in the 1960s, recalls: 'Every evening was endless entertainment. You had to make a positive decision not to take part. Except then we ran into a big storm and everything was cancelled because virtually no-one except me was on their feet'.

On the newly commissioned *Queen Mary* in 1936, the first big storm came as a dreadful shock. At one point she rolled 30 degrees. The furniture was not lashed down but it was too dangerous to go into the rooms to rescue it. In one panelled room, the upright piano, a Challen, was screwed down but tore from its screws. By the time the storm had abated and it was safe to enter, the piano had completely demolished the panelling and was itself reduced to its iron frame. There were no handrails in the ship at that time and many passengers broke bones. As well as relatives and well-wishers, twenty-seven ambulances met the ship at Southampton. Later the *Queen Mary* had stabilizers fitted but a passenger from the 1950s remembers 'the boat pitching and tossing and the main rooms having ropes you could grab if the weather became particularly rough'.

A passenger on the *Chusan* in the Atlantic in 1960s with her two children experienced winds of hurricane force: 'When they were up, all the babies and toddlers had to go in the playpen together in the nursery. It was the only place that was safe for them. In the evening, things seemed a bit better so the entertainment programme continued in the ballroom. Then the ship rolled hard. We all slid down in our chairs into the other side of the audience and then as she righted herself and rolled again, they all slid into us. What a mess'.

Nowadays, when practically all voyages are cruises, itineraries are arranged so that rough weather is avoided. Passengers fly the notorious North Atlantic and the Bay of Biscay to join their ship. Rather than suffer malnutrition as a result of seasickness, you are probably more likely to increase your propensity towards obesity.

Let's assume that the night is calm, dinner is long finished and the cabaret or show is over. It's time for a nightcap and then a last stroll on deck. Perhaps there are stars overhead, the smell of the sea drifts on the air, the gentle purr of the ship's engines hardly disturbs one of the last utterly peaceful places that it is possible to find.

Menu, *Atlantis*, 1931,
Royal Mail Lines.

## ABOUT THE RECIPES

Before you start cooking, here are a few guidelines about the recipes that follow. I would like to stress that these are my adaptations of recipes, many of which are classics. I tried to find at least two or three versions of each dish, some of which varied widely; I then wrote them up in my own words. They have all been tested. I was lucky enough to be assisted by enthusiastic volunteers, who not only followed the recipes to the letter but then filled in a questionnaire so that together we have honed them to a point where they should be a success.

There is one caveat: the recipes are written to feed four to six people according to appetite. They do not lend themselves to reducing down. If you want to cook them for two, make the recipe in the quantity given and enjoy the rest at another meal. There are a few recipes where quantities are for two and this is made clear in the recipe itself.

Some of the testers felt that the recipes had more butter, cream and sugar than we use today. However, by their nature many of these recipes are either for special occasions or entertaining. On such occasions, we do still spoil ourselves a little, so this is the ideal time to cook them.

Measures are given in metric and imperial. Where American measures differ from European, the equivalent is the third measurement given. The teaspoon and tablespoons mentioned are the standard measuring set sold in all kitchen shops.

When it comes to the cocktails, amounts are given in parts. Different people have different ideas about the size of their drinks. I hope this method of measuring allows for that.

Eggs are all standard size 3. I have given a tin size or indicated the approximate size of pan needed for the recipes. I have given cooking times and oven temperatures, but please, please use them as an indication not an order. I have found from personal experience that every oven varies. Where cakes and sponge puddings are concerned, for instance, the best test is to plunge a stainless steel skewer into the centre of the cake or pudding – if it comes out clean, the cake or pudding is cooked. When re-heating dishes, be sure to heat them right through until they are bubbling and too hot to eat straightaway.

Special occasion menus from Cunard and P&O.

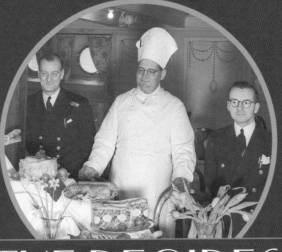

# THE RECIPES

'The art of dining well is no slight art,
the pleasure not a slight pleasure.'

MICHEL DE MONTAIGNE, FRENCH ESSAYIST 1533-1592

# 1 ▷ SOUPS

'Soup of the evening, beautiful soup', sang the Mock Turtle in Lewis Carroll's *Alice in Wonderland*. On the liners, it was soup at luncheon as well.

Every menu began with soup. There were usually at least two per menu, one thick and one clear, a vegetable purée or a velouté, and a consommé. The *Normandie*, whose menu consistently outdid all the others, had no less than five on the dinner menu. It is not difficult to understand why. In every galley, someone, probably a commis or junior chef would have been in charge of making stock, veal, beef and chicken. Fish stock or 'fumet' would also be made, probably daily. The French name for stock is *fond*, which means 'base' in English, and this is exactly what stock is – the base for nearly all soups and sauces.

What a spectacular variety of soups they made from the stock/*fond*. Many of them were classic recipes from the French tradition. Their names conjure up the era of rich, leisurely dining. Some were named after battles, for example Potage Creçy after the Battle of Creçy, which was fought on the rich agricultural fields of northern France. These fields were particularly famous for their carrots, the main ingredient. Velouté Marengo is a rich chicken soup. Originally, Napoleon's cook, presumably battle-worn after the Battle of Marengo, put together a scratch supper from the ingredients available. Solferino was a particularly bloody conflict between the French and the Austrians in 1859. I have chosen Potage Solferino as a recipe partly because I loved the idea of carrot and potato cannon balls and partly because it appeared on menus from the earliest to the latest.

An astonishing number are named after beautiful women. Several of them were French Royal mistresses. Crème Dubarry is named after Madame Dubarry, mistress to Louis XV. Cauliflower is the main ingredient: it reminded Vincent de la Chapelle, the chef who first created it, of her white wig. Incidentally, another of Louis' mistresses, Madame de Pompadour, inspired Potage Pompadour. Crème Montespan is named after Louis XIV's long-time love, Françoise Athenée de Rochechouart, Marquise de Montespan. Agnes Sorel, Dame de Beauté, in the fifteenth century inspired the legendary chef Taillevent to create not only soups but also sauces in her memory. I loved the idea of Consommé Aurore. *Aurore* is the French word for daybreak. The recipe calls for ham and carrots to be steeped in consommé colouring it a clear pale red, the colour of a rosy dawn.

So how was I to choose which soups to feature? I decided to look at those that were the most popular. I found several that were mentioned throughout the years. One was Croûte au Pot, a deceptively simple, clear broth containing fresh, diced vegetables, poured at the last minute over crisp croûtons, which was both refreshing and sustaining. Another was Mulligatawny, made by Indian cooks for their western masters, and served on all the liners not just those going to and from the Orient. A long-standing favourite was Potage St Germain, sometimes on the menu as Potage Longchamps or Potage Lamballe or as plain Pea Soup but always with green peas as the main ingredient. My recipe for Potage St Germain includes spinach as well.

St Andrew's Day or Hogmanay was always the occasion for a special Scottish menu. Scotland has given the world two wonderful soups, Cock-a-Leekie Soup and Scotch Broth, which appeared on some menus as Potage Écossaise. I decided one of these must go in, so I chose Cock-a-Leekie.

Chilled soups featured on many menus. The majority were variations on Consommé en Gelée – cold jellied consommé with different garnishes – but I decided to include Vichyssoise, a great favourite on the liners. It was created in 1919 by Louis Diat, the French Chef at the Hotel Carlton in New York and named after Vichy, the nearest town to his grandmother's garden where she grew the leeks and potatoes which are the basic ingredients. Gazpacho, the other chilled soup is a personal favourite.

The soups can be made in advance and reheated. They will all freeze, except the Gazpacho. If you are eating them within two or three days, they will keep in a covered container in the refrigerator.

I have included some recipes that appeared as starters, but have grouped these under The Cold Table section. They are interchangeable as starters or dishes on a cold buffet or even as a light lunch or supper. Soups were always offered as a first course, never the main course, but all these recipes will make a delicious light main meal.

# Cock-a-Leekie Soup

This is an old Scottish recipe that was served as an alternative to Scotch Broth on Burns Night or St Andrew's Night, or, as I found it, to 'Tattie Soup wi' Oatcakes' on a Scottish Landfall Dinner on the *Moldavia* the night before docking in Scotland. The date was Tuesday, 22 June 1937; the menu had 'Auld Lang Syne' on the back and various passengers had autographed it. I wonder if they did meet again after the voyage. On a practical note, it would be a good recipe to cook while also preparing the Pork Terrine With Chicken on page 98 since that uses the breasts of a chicken. The rest of the bird can be used in this recipe.

675 g/1 lb 8 oz leeks

Leg and wing joints of a chicken plus its carcass

3 rashers of bacon, chopped

Mixed bunch of parsley and thyme

Bay leaf

Salt and pepper to taste

100 g/4 oz/1½ cups stoned prunes

Wash and chop all the leeks except one. Put the leg and wing joints and the chicken carcass in a large saucepan, together with the leeks, bacon and herbs. Cover well with water. Bring to the boil, cover the pan, turn down the heat and simmer for at least 1 hour until the chicken is tender. Season to taste, then strain off the liquid picking out the chicken meat and cutting it into pieces. Put the broth and the chicken pieces back in the saucepan. Chop the remaining leek and add together with the prunes. Simmer very gently for 15 minutes and serve very hot.

Scottish Landfall Dinner, *Moldavia*, 1937, P&O.

# Crème Vichyssoise

450 g/1 lb leeks, white part only
(approx. 6 large leeks)

1 stick of celery

450 g/1 lb potatoes

50 g/2 oz/4 tablespoons butter

1 tablespoon chopped parsley

1.2 litres/2 pints/4½ cups strong
chicken stock

Salt and pepper to taste

300 ml/10 fl oz/¼ cup single
cream to serve

1 tablespoon chopped chives
to serve

The last dinner of a voyage is called The Farewell Dinner and is always a special occasion. The atmosphere is celebratory yet tinged with the knowledge that tomorrow brings change, a return to the real world. Behind the scenes, the chefs and kitchen staff know that this is a last chance to impress. Crème Vichyssoise, a rich, creamy mixture of leeks, potato, chicken broth and cream, served chilled, has always been 'special occasion' food. I found it on a Farewell Dinner Menu from the *Queen Mary* on Sunday, 7 August 1938.

Cut the leeks in half lengthways, slice finely and wash well. Chop the celery finely. Peel the potatoes and cut into small dice. Melt the butter in a large saucepan. Add the leeks and sauté very gently until soft and transparent. Stir frequently and do not allow them to brown. Add the celery, potatoes, parsley and chicken stock, cover the pan, and simmer until the vegetables are soft (about 30 minutes). Allow to cool slightly.

Put the soup through a blender or food processor and then use a wooden spoon to rub the purée through a sieve. It should be very smooth. Leave to cool, then chill until very cold in the refrigerator. Serve in individual soup plates or bowls. Just before serving, stir a tablespoon of cream, gently, into each bowl (you should be able to see the swirl), then sprinkle with finely chopped chives.

# Croûte au Pot

I found Croûte au Pot on the Luncheon Menus during sea trials on the *Titanic* in April 1912, and on the *Lusitania* in September 1913, on a Farewell Dinner on the *Kenya Castle* before arriving at Cape Town on 2 July 1958 and a Dinner Menu on the *Queen Mary* on 28 February 1966. A delicate broth with fresh vegetables and croûtes – rounds of crisp bread – it is a perfect start to a rich meal. And the main ingredient is always to hand. Every professional galley would have had its *pot au feu* simmering away creating the stock to serve as the foundation for soups and sauces. Cooks today are not at home enough to simmer bones and carcasses for long hours to make first stock and then consommé (consommé is a clear soup). I am suggesting you buy fresh consommé, which you will find in the chill cabinet of the supermarket.

Slice the baguette into rounds. You need about three or four per person, plus extras for seconds. Brush each side with olive oil and bake in a hot oven until crisp and golden. Keep an eye on them; they will toast very quickly. Pour the consommé into a saucepan and heat gently. Peel the onion, turnip and carrot. Cut all the vegetables into small neat dice. Add to the consommé with the garlic. Bring to the boil and immediately reduce the heat. Cover the pan and simmer until the vegetables are cooked but still have a bite to them. To peel the tomato, cut a circle through the skin and immerse in boiling water for approximately 2 minutes. Allow to cool slightly. The skin should peel off quite easily; if not, give it a minute more in the boiling water. De-seed and finely dice the flesh and add with the parsley. Place two or three croûtes in each shallow soup plate and fill with soup. Serve piping hot.

1 thin baguette

Olive oil

1.2 litres/2 pints/4½ cups fresh beef or chicken consommé/bouillon

1 onion

1 small turnip or parsnip

1 carrot

1 leek

1 stick of celery

1 garlic clove, crushed

1 large tomato

1 tablespoon finely chopped parsley

◇

# Gazpacho

50 g/2 oz /1 cup white bread torn up and without crusts

675 g/1 lb 8 oz ripe tomatoes

2 large green peppers

½ cucumber

½ Spanish onion

3 tablespoons white wine vinegar

2 tablespoons extra virgin olive oil

600 ml/1 pint/2¾ cups iced water

Salt and pepper to taste

### For the garnishes

2 tomatoes, skinned

1 green pepper

¼ Spanish onion

¼ cucumber, peeled

2 hardboiled eggs

2 slices of white bread, crusts removed

2 tablespoons olive oil

**A Spanish Dinner Fiesta was held on the *Queen Mary* on Monday, 14 March 1966. The soup offered was this wonderfully simple and refreshing dish, which always tastes to me like 'liquid summer' when the garnishes are added. There is no better start to dinner on a hot day. This has to be made in a blender or a food processor and you need to leave time to chill it before serving.**

Soak the bread in water while you are preparing the vegetables. Cut the tomatoes into quarters. Remove the stalks and seeds from the peppers and cut into chunks. Peel the cucumber and onion and cut into chunks. Remove the bread from the water. Put all the vegetables and bread into the food processor or blender together with the vinegar, oil and water. You will have to do this in batches. Reduce each batch to a pulp. Push the pulp through a sieve with a wooden spoon to produce a pale pink, thinnish liquid. It should be very smooth. Taste it, and season with salt and pepper. It may need a little more water. Chill until required.

While the soup is chilling, prepare the garnishes as follows. Chop the vegetables finely and place each one in a separate small bowl. Chop the hardboiled eggs and put in a small bowl. Cut the bread into dice, fry until golden in the oil and place in a small bowl. Serve with the soup and allow each person to add their own garnish.

# Mulligatawny Soup

Mulligatawny Soup takes its name from the Indian word *Mulagatannir*. This is a 'pepper water', a spice and onion infusion that used to be the basis of the soup. It is a legacy of the British Empire, a recipe concocted by Indian cooks for their British masters and mistresses. It uses Indian ingredients but in a way that appeals to western tastes. It was a great favourite: I found it on many menus including a Fancy Dress Dinner on the *Stratheden* on 16 February 1949 and a Luncheon Menu on the *Queen Mary* on Saturday, 12 October 1963.

Heat the oil in a saucepan large enough to take all the ingredients and gently fry the onion and garlic for five minutes. Add the lentils, tomatoes, chilli, tomato purée, stock, cloves, curry paste and raisins. Stir well, bring to the boil, turn down the heat and simmer for 40 minutes. Purée half the soup in a blender or food processor and return to the pan. This gives a thick purée but still with some texture. Season to taste with salt and pepper, add the coconut milk and lime juice and zest, and reheat if necessary. Hand round the lime segments with the bowls of soup so that each person can squeeze the lime over the top.

3 tablespoons olive oil

1 medium onion, peeled and chopped

3 garlic cloves, chopped

110 g/4 oz/½ cup red lentils

225 g/8 oz tomatoes, de-seeded and chopped

1 chilli, finely chopped

1 tablespoon tomato purée

1.5 litres/2½ pints/5 cups chicken stock

4 cloves

1 tablespoon mild curry paste

50 g/2 oz/1/3 cup raisins

Salt and pepper to taste

200 ml/7 fl oz/1 cup coconut milk

Grated zest and juice of 1 lime

Lime segments to garnish

# Onion Soup au Gratin

450 g/1 lb onions

75 g/3 oz/6 tablespoons unsalted butter

1 teaspoon sugar

1.2 litres/2 pints/4½ cups vegetable stock

½ level teaspoon salt

French Baguette, cut into 1 cm/½ in. thick slices

50 g/2 oz Gruyère cheese, finely grated

25 g/1 oz/¼ cup plain flour

Onion soup au Gratin appears on many breakfast menus. I found it on the *Saxonia* on Thursday, 31 August 1961. Although today it may more likely be served as a lunch or supper dish, it was originally associated with the early morning wholesale fruit and vegetable market at Les Halles in Paris. The porters there kept out the morning chill by drinking huge mugs of the soup.

Preheat the oven to 160°C/350°F/Gas Mark 4. Peel and slice the onions. Melt 50 g/2 oz/4 tablespoons of the butter in a large saucepan. Add the onions and the sugar and sauté gently until the onions are soft and transparent, continue frying until they are golden brown. This will probably take between 20 and 30 minutes. Stir in the stock and salt, cover the pan and simmer for 30 minutes. While the soup is simmering prepare the croûtes. Butter both sides of the bread slices with the rest of the butter, scatter the top side with a little cheese and bake in the oven until the bread is crisp. Mix the flour separately with a little of the liquid from the soup until thoroughly blended. Stir the mixture into the soup and bring back to the boil. Simmer for 2 to 3 minutes until the soup has thickened.

Put one slice of bread in each bowl before filling the bowl with soup and serve the remaining croûtes and grated cheese in separate bowls.

# Potage Solferino

**Potage Solferino was an enduring favourite. Passengers enjoyed this soup at luncheon on the *Soudan* in 1903 and at a Farewell Dinner on board the *Ausonia* in 1935.**

The Battle of Solferino between France and Austria occurred on 24 June 1859. The heavy casualties both during and after the conflict led to the foundation of the Red Cross and so a chef invented a potato and tomato dish in the colours of the Red Cross. The optional garnish of balls of cooked carrots and potatoes represent cannon balls!

Melt half the butter in a large saucepan. Add the onion and leeks and sauté gently until soft, but do not brown. Add the tomatoes, stock, garlic and potatoes. Bring to the boil, then reduce the heat and simmer gently until all the vegetables are soft. Purée the mixture in a food processor or blender. Rinse out the pan, return the purée to it and bring to the boil. Stir in the rest of the butter, chopped into small pieces. Season to taste with salt and pepper.

For the garnish, peel the carrot and potato and boil until tender. Make cannon balls with a melon baller and float several of these in each bowl. Serve the soup with a swirl of crème fraîche or yoghurt.

30 g/1½ oz/3 tablespoons butter

1 medium onion, peeled and diced

2 leeks, white part only, chopped and washed

5 medium tomatoes, de-seeded and chopped coarsely

1 litre /1¾ pints/4 cups chicken or vegetable stock (the better the quality, the better the soup)

2 garlic cloves, peeled and chopped

250 g/8 oz potatoes, peeled and diced

Salt and pepper to taste

### For the garnish (optional)

1 large carrot

1 potato

Crème fraîche or yoghurt to serve

Luncheon Menu, *Soudan*, 1903, P&O.

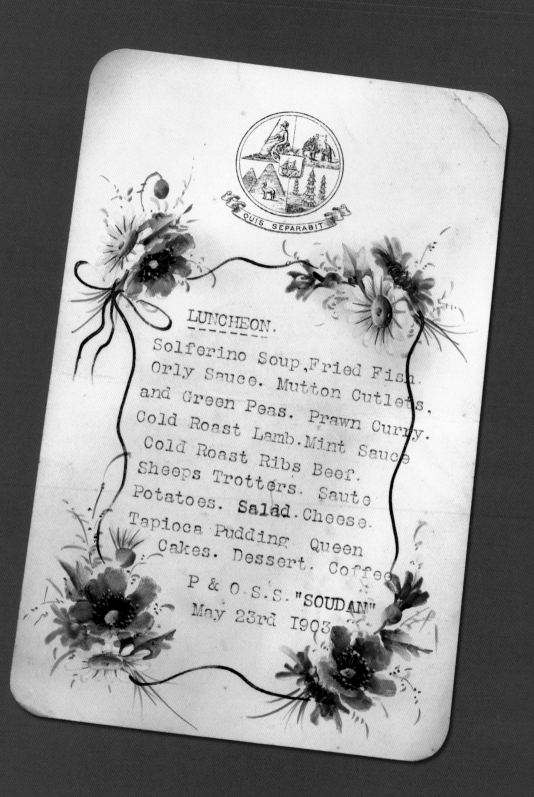

QUIS SEPARABIT

LUNCHEON.
----------
Solferino Soup,Fried Fish.
Orly Sauce. Mutton Cutlets,
and Green Peas. Prawn Curry.
Cold Roast Lamb.Mint Sauce
Cold Roast Ribs Beef.
Sheeps Trotters. Saute
Potatoes. **Salad**.Cheese.
Tapioca Pudding. Queen
Cakes. Dessert. Coffee

P & O S S. "SOUDAN"
May 23rd 1903

# Potage St Germain

Potage St Germain or Green Pea Soup appeared on the menu of the ill-fated *Lusitania* on Saturday, 13 September 1913, a year before she was torpedoed off the coast of Ireland. I found it again on the Luncheon Menu of the *Queen Elizabeth* forty-five years later, on Saturday, 12 April 1958. It has a rich, creamy taste and a beautiful colour. I like it with a little texture left in it, but if you prefer it completely smooth, then push the mixture through a sieve after processing and before re-heating.

Wash the spinach, lettuce and leeks. Shred finely and put in a saucepan large enough to take all the ingredients. Add the peas, salt, sugar, butter and water. Bring to the boil, reduce the heat and simmer for approximately 15 minutes. Take off the heat and add the stock. Process the mixture and return to the pan to reheat before serving. Check the seasoning and add more salt and some freshly ground pepper before serving piping hot with a swirl of cream.

25 g/1 oz spinach leaves

1 small head of lettuce (Romaine or Midget Gem is best)

2 leeks, green part only

500 g/1 lb 2 oz frozen green peas, or fresh peas if available

1 level teaspoon salt

1 heaped teaspoon sugar

50 g/2 oz/4 tablespoons butter

150 ml/5 fl oz/½ cup water

1.2 litres/2 pints/4½ cups chicken or vegetable stock

Salt and pepper to taste

Single cream to serve

Menu, *Lusitania*, 1913, Cunard.

# FISH AND MEAT

2

'The food was superb, the quantity overcame you.'

I felt rather the same as this passenger, who travelled regularly to and from Europe in the 1950s, when I started looking through the menus. From the smallest to the largest, Dinner or Luncheon, there are never less than three main dishes on every menu, whether it was an emigrant ship in 1914, a troopship in 1941, Tourist Class to the East or First Class on the great ships plying the North Atlantic. On many menus there were ten or more hot main dishes. How was I to choose? I decided to eliminate those dishes that we might find difficult to source today, such as this Tête de Veau: 'Boned and trimmed Calf's Head, cooked lightly in thickened White Stock with Vegetables and Bouquet Garni. Served with Madeira Sauce flavoured with Turtle, Herbs, garnished with diced Olives, Ox Tongue and Mushrooms, also with Vinaigrette Sauce'.

That decided, I started with the fish course. All First-Class menus served one; so did most Tourist-Class. Salmon, turbot, lobster, Dover sole, scallops, all the choicest fish from the sea were there. Fish needs the lightest of cooking: broiling, grilling and poaching were the preferred methods. The fish was then served with a variety of sauces. They have splendid names, such as Ambassade, Caprice, Carmen, Judic and Ravigote. I soon discovered these sauces were sourced from the classic French chef's cuisine and that the ingredients and the methods might be difficult for a domestic kitchen. So I have chosen fish dishes that translate well to today's tastes and methods: a Fish Chowder, Grilled Turbot Niçoise and from the East, a Goan Fish Curry.

There were always roasts of all kinds with their appropriate garnishes: Roast Ribs or Sirloin of Beef with Yorkshire Pudding, Roast Turkey with Cranberry Sauce, Roast Lamb with Mint Sauce to name but a few. There were often grills to choose from as well: steaks, lamb chops, pork cutlets. I found myself counting the number of ways used to describe a hamburger: Boeuf Haché, Salisbury Steak, Ground Beef and Chopped Beef were some of them. However, in all these dishes, the heat of the oven and the quality of the meat is more important than the finesse of the cook, so I chose to include dishes where spicing and other ingredients compliment the meat.

Some, such as Salmi of Game, Boeuf à la Mode, Navarin of Lamb Printanier, and Le Caneton à l'Orange are again, from French cuisine. Buy the best ingredients you can afford, cook them with care and these dishes will taste wonderful. Other dishes, such as Steak, Kidney and Mushroom Pie and Irish Stew are homely British favourites. Again, quality and care will produce a delicious result.

Perhaps this is the moment to give curry a special mention. Both passengers and crew remember the curries as something special. Curry and Rice – we are often not told what is in it – appears on all the various menus for First Class, Tourist and Second Class, for troops during the Second World War, even on a Breakfast Menu for emigrants going to Australia in 1915. It was never served in the evening, a gesture to digestion presumably.

There's a delicious Butterbean, Spinach and Potato Curry on page 86, but in this chapter you will find Curry and Rice Madras and Goan Fish Curry. I just had to include a recipe from Goa, which has a long and distinguished connection with the galleys and dining rooms of the liners. Goanese stewards and cooks are mentioned with affection from the earliest accounts of passages to this recent comment: 'On the way to South Africa in January 2002, we had a Goanese crew and not only was there a different curry on the menu every day, but one evening we had a special curry feast which was wonderful.'

Left: Chefs preparing breakfast, *Windsor Castle*, c. 1960, Union-Castle.

Opposite: Menu, *Laconia*, 1929, Cunard.

Cunard
Line

# Grilled Turbot Niçoise

I found Grilled Turbot Niçoise on the Dinner Menu of the *Iberia* on Wednesday, 13 June 1962. The *Iberia* was the new flagship of P&O and serving fish with a sauce that originated in southern France was up-to-the minute cuisine of the time. The city of Nice is famous for its dishes using fresh vegetables stewed gently in olive oil. The fishmonger had no turbot the day I cooked this. He recommended brill; it was delicious. I have turned the original sauce into a vegetable accompaniment. Serve with steamed new potatoes, or, if you want to enjoy the fish and vegetables as the French do, a crisp French loaf.

Preheat the oven to 200°C/400°F/Gas Mark 6. Either shake flour over the fish fillets on both sides or spread the flour on a plate and coat the fish with it. Brush the flour-coated fillets with 1 tablespoon of the olive oil. Arrange on a roasting pan covered with baking parchment.

Melt the rest of the oil in a shallow pan. Trim, chop and wash the leek, peel and chop the garlic and tomatoes. Sauté the leek gently in the pan. When it is soft add the garlic and tomatoes. Season with the sugar, salt and pepper and cook very gently for approximately 15 minutes.

This is probably about the right moment to put the fillets in the oven. They take about 10 minutes to cook. Trim the beans and steam or cook in boiling, salted water for about 10 minutes. They should still have some bite to them. Add to the leek and tomato mixture, stir round so they are well blended; cook for a further 5 minutes.

You can cook the vegetables ahead of time. They taste just as good at room temperature or lukewarm. Either way, serve the fillets hot from the oven and the vegetables with the fish.

2 fillets of turbot or brill per person (ask the fishmonger to fillet the fish for you)

Flour in a flour shaker or 2 tablespoons of flour

4 tablespoons best olive oil (the better the oil, the better the flavour)

1 large leek

2 cloves of garlic

225 g/8 oz tomatoes

1 teaspoon of sugar

Salt and pepper to taste

225 g/8 oz green beans

CAÏQUES—Eastern Mediterranean

P&O

MENU

# Goan Fish Curry

1 fresh chilli (if you like your food spicy, add more)

2 teaspoons coriander seeds

2 teaspoons cumin seeds

1 teaspoon paprika

1 teaspoon turmeric

3 garlic cloves, peeled

2 cm/1 in. piece of fresh ginger, peeled

Water as necessary

3 tablespoons vegetable oil

1 medium onion, finely chopped

2 medium tomatoes, chopped

200 ml/7 fl oz/½ cup water

200 ml/7 fl oz/½ cup coconut milk

675 g/1 lb 8 oz firm white fish, cut into chunks (cod, monkfish or hake are all suitable)

Salt and pepper to taste

1 tablespoon tamarind pulp (available in small jars from the supermarket)

1 tablespoon chopped fresh coriander leaves

**This curry featured on the *Chusan* menu on Wednesday, 4 January 1961 as she steamed south to Australia across the Indian Ocean, and it was probably served by Goan stewards. An essential ingredient is coconut milk.**

Process the chilli, coriander and cumin seeds, paprika and turmeric to a powder. Add the garlic, ginger and sufficient water and process again to make a paste.

Heat the oil in a wok or pan large enough to take all the ingredients. Add the onion and cook until it is golden brown. Reduce the heat, add the tomatoes and cook for another 5 minutes. Stir in the spice paste and cook for a few minutes. Add the water and coconut milk, bring to the boil and then simmer for 5 minutes. Add the fish and cook gently for 5 minutes. Season and stir in the tamarind pulp carefully so as not to break up the fish and cook for 3 minutes. Serve immediately garnished with chopped coriander. Steamed rice is a good accompaniment.

Opposite: Menu, *Oriana*, 1962, P&O.

# Salmon Fishcakes

I found Salmon Fishcakes on the Tourist-Class Luncheon Menu of the *Windsor Castle* when she was steaming from Capetown to Southampton on Wednesday, 17 August 1977. The fishcakes at that time may have been made with tinned salmon; the recipe outlined below uses fresh, which is readily available.

Steam the salmon until cooked (approximately 10 minutes). Place in a mixing bowl and flake, removing any bones. Allow to cool. Add the mashed potato, spring onions, parsley and lemon zest and juice. Stir in the beaten egg and season to taste. The mixture is quite soft but if you wet your hands before forming the cakes it will not stick so much. Spread the flour on a plate and as you make each cake (the mixture will make eight small or four large fishcakes) roll it in flour mixed with a little extra seasoning. Heat the butter and oil in a large frying pan and fry the cakes on each side until crisp and golden.

Serve immediately with a wedge of lemon.

225 g/8 oz salmon fillet

450 g/1 lb potatoes, peeled, cooked, mashed and cooled

2 tablespoons spring onions, finely chopped

2 tablespoons parsley, finely chopped

Finely grated zest and juice of half a lemon

1 egg, well beaten

2 tablespoons plain flour

Salt and pepper to taste

25 g/1 oz/2 tablespoons butter

2 tablespoons olive oil

Remaining half a lemon to garnish

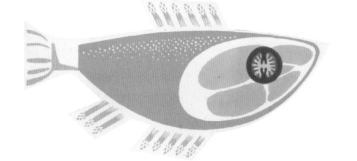

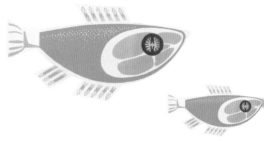

# Fish Chowder

50 g/2 oz/4 tablespoons butter

50 g/2 oz/¼ cup ham or bacon lardons

1 medium onion

2 sticks of celery

1 large carrot

850 ml/1½ pints/3½ cups vegetable stock

150 g/6 oz firm white fish (cod or monkfish are both suitable)

150 g/6 oz salmon fillet

150 ml/5 fl oz/⅔ cup single cream

110 g/4 oz/⅔ cup large peeled and cooked prawns

2 tablespoons chopped parsley or dill

**Fish Chowder Manhattan was on the Luncheon Menu of the *Queen Elizabeth* on Friday, 11 April 1958. Boston Clam Chowder was on the Luncheon Menu of the *Queen Mary* on Friday, 11 October 1963. There were always more fish dishes on the menus on Fridays. American passengers would have appreciated this traditional East Coast dish. I have chosen a chowder that uses a mixture of white fish and salmon, not clams as these are more difficult to find in Britain. Light yet substantial, this needs no further accompaniment than steamed or boiled new potatoes or crusty bread.**

Melt the butter in a large saucepan or sauté pan. Fry the ham or bacon lardons until they are crisp. Remove and drain on paper towels. Peel and slice the onion, chop the celery into small chunks, peel and cut the carrot into batons. Sauté all the vegetables for a minute or two in the butter, then add the stock. Bring to the boil, then turn down the heat and simmer with the lid on until the vegetables are cooked, but are still a little crisp. The chowder can be prepared ahead of time to this point.

Just before you want to serve the chowder, cut the white fish and salmon into chunks. Lay on top of the vegetable mixture to steam as you reheat the chowder gently until bubbling. Do not stir. Turn off the heat, add the cream, scatter the prawns, cooked lardons and parsley on top and serve immediately.

# Boeuf à la Mode

This classic dish not only tastes wonderful but the aroma when it is cooking tempts the most jaded appetite. It must have been the perfect dish for the chefs on the liners. It will happily sit and wait until you are ready to eat it. Dress it up with small sweet onions and tiny carrots. All it then needs is mashed or new potatoes and the best bottle of wine you can afford. Boeuf or Braised Beef à la Mode appeared on the Luncheon Menu on the *Queen Elizabeth* on Saturday, 12 April 1958.

Ideally the meat should be marinated for 6 to 24 hours before cooking. However, if you don't have time, pour the marinade items into the casserole after browning the meat. The classic recipe calls for pigs' trotters. These can be quite difficult to track down but a good butcher should have them. Ask him to split them for you. If you can't find them, don't worry; the dish will still taste fantastic.

Place half the vegetables, herbs and spices in a large bowl. Rub the meat with the salt and pepper and place it on top. Cover with the rest of the vegetables, herbs and spices. Pour on the wine, brandy and olive oil. Cover the bowl and marinate for at least 6 hours and up to 24 hours, turning the meat in the marinade from time to time.

Half an hour before you intend to start cooking, remove the meat and dry thoroughly on paper towels. Let it rest for half an hour or so. Set aside the marinade. Preheat the oven to 150°C/300°F/Gas Mark 2.

Heat two tablespoons of oil in a cast iron casserole until it is nearly smoking. Brown the meat on all sides. Add the split pigs' trotters and brown them, then pour out any fat remaining. Pour in all the marinade. Add the lardons. At this point the liquid should come about two-thirds of the way up the beef joint. Bring up to simmering point on the top of the stove. Cover the casserole and place in the oven and cook gently for approximately 2½ hours.

110 g/4 oz onions, peeled and thinly sliced

110 g/4 oz carrots, peeled and thinly sliced

110 g/4 oz celery, diced

2 garlic cloves, peeled and halved

2 bay leaves

2 whole cloves

4 tablespoons chopped parsley

1 teaspoon mixed herbs, preferably Herbes de Provence

1.3 kg/3 lb piece of beef (topside is fine, sirloin is the best)

1 dessertspoon salt

Freshly ground pepper

1 bottle of red wine

Small glass of brandy

150 ml/5 fl oz/¾ cup olive oil

2 tablespoons oil

2 pigs trotters, split (optional)

110 g/4 oz/½ cup lardons or chopped streaky bacon

**For the garnish**

450 g/1 lb small onions or shallots

450 g/1 lb tiny whole carrots or large carrots

300 ml/10 fl oz/1½ cups beef stock

1 dessertspoon sugar

The cooking time may vary according to the cut of meat. Sirloin, for instance, needs less time than topside. Turn the meat a couple of times during the cooking time.

While the meat is cooking, peel the onions or shallots and the carrots for the garnish. Cut the carrots into thick batons. Heat the beef stock with the sugar and simmer the onions and carrots gently for approximately 15 minutes. They should be cooked but still have a bite to them. When the meat is tender, lift the joint from the casserole on to a carving dish and remove any strings, etc. Keep it warm while you finish the sauce and vegetables. Strain the juices in the casserole into a saucepan and reheat. Boil rapidly to reduce the liquid for 5 minutes. Adjust the seasoning, add the braised onions and carrots and simmer a couple of minutes longer.

Pour a little of the sauce over the meat, carve it at the table and serve with vegetables and sauce from the casserole.

Approaching Corfu, c. 1935.

# Navarin of Lamb Printanier

**Navarin of Lamb Printanier was on the menu for lunch on Tuesday, 15 April 1958 on the *Queen Elizabeth*. Nobody can decide whether this classic French dish is named after the Battle of Navarino during the Greek War of Independence in 1827 or after the *navets* (turnips) which were originally the main accompanying vegetable. April is the right month because traditionally it uses the tender new lamb and the tiny new vegetables that are available in early summer. Nowadays, with freezers and air freight, we can make it at any time of year, but it is still particularly sweet tasting made in the spring.**

Preheat the oven to 180°C/350°F/Gas Mark 4. Cut the meat into large dice. Dry the meat with paper towels before browning a few pieces at a time in the oil in a frying pan. As the pieces are browned, place in a large cast iron casserole. Sprinkle the lamb with the sugar and toss over a moderately high heat for 3 or 4 minutes until the sugar has caramelized. This will give a fine amber colour to the sauce. Toss the meat next with the salt, pepper and flour. Place the casserole uncovered in the middle of the hot oven for 5 minutes. Remove, toss the meat again and return the casserole to the oven for another 5 minutes. This browns the flour evenly and coats the lamb with a light crust. Take out the casserole and turn the oven down to 140°C/275°F/Gas Mark 3.

Pour the fat out of the frying pan. Pour in the stock and bring to the boil. Pour into the casserole. On the top of the stove bring to simmering point, then add the garlic, tomatoes, rosemary and bay leaves. If there is not sufficient stock to cover the meat, add more. The meat should be almost covered by the liquid. Put the lid on the casserole and place back in the oven. Regulate the heat so that the casserole simmers slowly for 1 hour.

1.3 kg/3 lb stewing lamb (ideally this should consist of some boneless and some lamb on the bone)

2 tablespoons olive oil

1 tablespoon granulated sugar

1 teaspoon salt

Freshly ground pepper

1 level tablespoon plain flour

600 ml/1 pint/3 cups vegetable stock

2 cloves of crushed garlic

350 g/12 oz tomatoes, peeled, seeded and chopped

Sprig of fresh rosemary

2 bay leaves

450 g/1 lb new potatoes, scraped clean

6 small carrots or 3 large carrots, peeled and cut into batons

12 small onions or shallots, peeled, with a cross cut in each base

12 small turnips

110 g/4 oz fresh French beans, cut into short pieces

110 g/4 oz/⅔ cup fresh or frozen petit pois

Chopped parsley to serve

Remove from the oven and pour the contents through a sieve placed over a bowl. Wash the casserole. Return the meat to the casserole minus any loose bones. Skim the fat off the sauce in the bowl, check and correct the seasoning and pour back over the meat. Add the potatoes, carrots, onions and turnips. Bring to simmering point on the top of the stove, then cover and return to the oven. Simmer the dish for another hour or until the meat and vegetables are tender when pierced with a knife.

While the casserole is simmering, cook the beans for 5 minutes in boiling, salted water. Add the peas for the final 2 minutes. Drain and run under cold water to set the colour.

Remove the casserole from the oven, add the beans and peas and simmer covered for a final 5 minutes on the top of the stove to incorporate them into the dish. Sprinkle chopped parsley over the casserole and serve.

Dinner on the *Transvaal Castle*, c. 1961, Union-Castle.

# Curry and Rice Madras

Curry and Rice is one of the very few dishes from non-European cuisines that appears on any of the menus. As it mostly appears simply as 'Curry and Rice', I can't tell how spicy it was or what meat was in the curry. It appears on the Bill of Fare of the *Iberia* as recorded by William Thackeray, travelling between Jaffa and Alexandria on 12 October 1844 and on the Luncheon Menu for Monday, 11 February 1929 on the *Laconia*, which was on a West Indies Cruise. Curry was invariably a Luncheon dish, when it was called 'Curry and Rice – Madras'. In Britain, Madras Curry has come to mean a medium hot curry, spicier than a Korma, less hot than a Vindaloo. I have chosen a traditional mutton/lamb curry recipe that uses freshly ground spices. Increase or decrease the number of chillies as your taste dictates.

Roast the chillies, cinnamon, cumin seeds and cloves together in a frying pan for 30 seconds. Then grind the spices in a pestle and mortar or blender to a powder. Heat the oil in a large pan. Add the onions and fry until they are golden, stirring from time to time. Stir in the ginger and garlic and cook for a further minute. Then add the paprika, turmeric, coriander and ground roasted spices. Stir well and pour in the coconut milk. Add the mutton or lamb, the water and the tomatoes. Bring to the boil, cover the pan and reduce the heat. Simmer gently for 45 to 50 minutes or until the meat is tender.

Season with salt and serve with Basmati Rice and Mango Chutney. Cucumber Raita – grated cucumber in yoghurt with fresh mint is a delicious cooling sambal or side dish.

---

4 dried birds eye chillies (you can substitute 1½ teaspoons chilli flakes)

10 cm/4 in. cinnamon bark

1 teaspoon cumin seeds

6 cloves

4 tablespoons vegetable oil

450 g/1 lb onions, peeled and finely sliced

2.5 cm/1 in. piece of fresh ginger, peeled and finely chopped

3 garlic cloves, peeled and finely chopped

1 teaspoon paprika

1 teaspoon turmeric

1 teaspoon ground coriander

400 ml/14 fl oz/1¾ cups tinned coconut milk

700 g/1 lb 8 oz boneless mutton or leg of lamb cut into 1 cm/½ in. cubes

425 ml/15 fl oz/2 cups water

225 g/8 oz/1 cup tomatoes, roughly chopped

Salt to taste

---

Menu, *German*, 1881,
Union Steam Ship Company.

# MENU.

### UNION STEAM SHIP COMPANY, LIMITED.

ESTABLISHED 1853.

## S.S. "GERMAN."

**Soup.**

Pea Soup.

**Fish.**

**Entrees.**

Cutlets de Poss

Canard Aux Petite Pois

**Removes.**

Roast Venison & Jelly.

Corned Beef. + Carrots.

Sheeps Head. Brain Sauce

**Releves.**

Madras Curry

French Beans Mashed Potatoes

**Pastry.**

Blanc Mange, Plum Pudding

Sandwich Pastry

**Dessert.**

Assorted

17th Feby 1881

# Steak, Kidney and Mushroom Pie

**This was on the Luncheon/Dejeuner Menu on the *Queen Mary* on Friday, 11 October 1963. The menu was listed in French on the left page and in English on the right. Steak and Kidney Pie was not translated. It stayed in English on both pages. Quite right too; it is one of the best dishes in English traditional cooking.**

Preheat the oven to 160°C/325°F/Gas Mark 3. Trim the steak and kidney and cut into cubes. Put the seasoned flour in a polythene bag and toss the meat in it until coated.

Melt half the butter in a frying pan. Peel and slice the onion and fry until soft and golden brown. Remove with a slotted spoon and put in a casserole, large enough to take the meat mixture. Melt the rest of butter and fry the flour-coated meat in the same pan until it is brown. Do this in batches so each piece has a chance to brown on all sides. Add to the onion in the casserole. Fry the mushrooms and mix with the meat and onions. Shake in any loose flour from the polythene bag. Cover with the wine and stock and add the bay leaf. Bring to the boil on the top of the stove then cover the casserole and cook gently in the oven until the meat is just tender. It should take about $1^1/_2$ hours. Let the mixture cool. The dish can be prepared well ahead of time to this point, even overnight if this is convenient as long as the filling is kept in the refrigerator.

Preheat the oven to 200°C/400°F/Gas Mark 6. Fill a large deep pie dish with the mixture. Stand a pie-funnel in the middle of the dish. Roll out the pastry and cut out a lid. You can use some of the pastry trimmings to line the edge of the dish under the lid, which will give you a nice thick edge. Use a fork to decorate the edge. Use the rest of the pastry trimmings to make leaf decorations for the top of the pie. Brush the lid and the decorations with the egg and milk. Bake for 20 minutes, then lower the temperature to 160°C/325°F/Gas Mark 3 and cook until the pastry is really crisp and brown.

900 g/2 lb best braising steak

225 g/8 oz lambs or ox kidney

1 level tablespoon flour seasoned with salt and pepper

75 g/3 oz/6 tablespoons butter

1 large onion

225 g/8 oz button mushrooms

200 ml/7 fl oz/¾ cup red wine

200 ml/7 fl oz/¾ cup beef or vegetable stock

Bay leaf

450 g/1 lb puff pastry

1 egg yolk mixed with a little milk

# Irish Stew

1 tablespoon vegetable oil

450 g/1 lb neck fillet of lamb, cut into chunks

1 large onion, peeled and sliced

2 medium carrots, peeled and cut into short lengths

1 stick of celery, chopped

350 g/12 oz new potatoes, scrubbed

Approximately ¾ litre/1¼ pints/3 cups vegetable stock

225 g/8 oz cooked potato, mashed

Salt and pepper to taste

Chopped parsley to garnish

**Served on the *Queen Mary* on 19 March 1966, this is the chef's own description: 'Choice succulent young Lamb, stewed with early Spring Vegetables and Potatoes until as thick as the Bogs of County Clare and nostalgic of the streets of Old Dublin'. It is a meal in itself, but Irish soda bread to soak up the gravy would be both authentic and delicious. The other traditional side dish is pickled red cabbage.**

Preheat the oven to 150°C/300°F/Gas Mark 2. Heat the oil in a cast-iron casserole and fry the meat and onions together until nicely browned. Take the casserole off the heat and add the carrots, the celery and the potatoes. Stir, and add the vegetable stock to cover the meat and vegetables. Bring the casserole to the boil, cover, and then either simmer very slowly on the top of the stove or stew gently in the oven until the meat is tender and the vegetables are cooked but still have a little crunch. Stir in the mashed potato to thicken the gravy, and season to taste with salt and pepper. Garnish with the parsley before serving.

St Patrick's Day Menu, *Queen Mary*, 1966, Cunard.

# Noisettes d'Agneau — Reform

**Served on the *Laconia* in February 1929 as a main course dinner dish, Noisettes, or Cutlets, Reform has a long history. The dish was invented for the very English Reform Club by Charles Francatelli, an Italian chef to Queen Victoria. He was a pupil of the famous French chef, Antonin Carème, who was chef to the Prince Regent, later George IV. Francatelli's original recipe involved frying the noisettes coated in ham and breadcrumbs and garnishing with Reform Chips – tiny batons of ham, hardboiled egg and truffles. I have suggested grilling the noisettes and have simplified the sauce and garnish.**

Finely dice the carrot, onion and gammon. Melt the butter and fry the vegetables and meat until golden brown. Add the wine vinegar and boil the mixture so that the liquid reduces rapidly. When it is about one third less, add the vegetable stock, redcurrant jelly, cloves, nutmeg and thyme. Simmer very slowly for 30 minutes. Put the arrowroot in a small bowl, add a tablespoon of the sauce and stir until it is smooth. Stir this mixture into the sauce and whisk or stir until smooth. It should thicken the sauce without colouring it. Strain the sauce into a basin and stand it in a saucepan of boiling water to keep warm while you grill the noisettes. Alternatively you can make the sauce ahead of time and reheat it gently when you need it.

Preheat the grill to a high heat. Brush the noisettes with oil and grill for approximately 5 minutes each side. Alternatively you can cook them in a heavy-ridged grill pan over a high heat.

Put a couple of dessertspoons of sauce on a heated plate, place two noisettes per person on the top and garnish with the Reform Chips and parsley. Serve with steamed or boiled new potatoes.

1 medium carrot

1 small onion

110 g/4 oz gammon or lean back bacon

25 g/1 oz/2 tablespoons butter

150 ml/5 fl oz/½ cup white wine vinegar

600 ml/1 pint/2½ cups vegetable stock

110 g/4 oz redcurrant jelly

4 cloves

Finely grated nutmeg to taste

1/2 teaspoon dried thyme

2 heaped teaspoons of arrowroot or cornflour

Noisettes of lamb (boned lamb chops each tied into a disk – allow two per person)

### For the garnish

Reform Chips: matchsticks of chopped cooked carrots, gherkins, hardboiled egg whites, ham

Chopped parsley

# Risotto with Chicken Livers

25 g/1 oz/2 tablespoons butter

3 tablespoons olive oil

1 large onion, peeled and chopped

2 sticks of celery, chopped

1 large carrot, peeled and diced

4 rashers of streaky bacon

275 g/12 oz/1¼ cups Arborio, or similar risotto rice

1 litre/1¾ pints/4 cups vegetable stock

450 g/1 lb chicken livers, chopped into bite-sized pieces

110 g/4 oz button mushrooms, cut into slices

**For the garnish**

25 g/1 oz/¼ cup pine nuts

2 tablespoons chopped parsley

Freshly-grated Parmesan cheese

**Risotto didn't appear in the early menus, but Italian dishes were beginning to feature by 1961. This was served on P&O's *Chusan* on New Year's Day 1961. The secret of good risotto is using the correct rice and regular stirring as you add the stock, little by little. The final dish should be very slightly soupy but the rice will still have a little bite to it. 'Al dente' say the Italians who like their pasta that way too.**

Heat the butter and oil in either a large frying pan with a lid or a wok. Gently sauté the onion, celery and carrot for five minutes. Chop the bacon in small pieces and add to the pan with the rice. Stir so that everything is well coated with butter and oil. Begin to add the stock slowly, about a cup at a time and stir as the rice mixture starts to absorb the stock. Keep adding and stirring until about half the stock has been absorbed. Then add the chicken livers. Stir into the risotto and continue to add the stock. The risotto will have absorbed all the stock by the time it is cooked. When the risotto has absorbed nearly all the stock, add the mushrooms. Cook for another 2 or 3 minutes.

Toast the pine nuts for a minute or two in a dry frying pan. Scatter over the top of the risotto with the parsley and Parmesan cheese just before serving.

# Corned Beef Hash

**Corned Beef Hash is comfort food rather than a dish designed to impress. It featured on the Luncheon Menu on the *Queen Mary* on a Las Palmas Easter Cruise on Tuesday, 1 March 1966.**

2 large mild onions

4 tablespoons olive oil

225 g/8 oz/1 cup tinned corned beef

450 g/1 lb peeled, boiled potatoes

Salt, freshly ground pepper and a dash of Worcester sauce, to taste

4 eggs

Peel and slice the onions. Heat 2 tablespoons of the oil in a large frying pan and fry the onions until they are soft and golden. Cut the beef into chunks, cut the potatoes into cubes and mix with the onions in a large bowl. Break everything up with a fork so that it is well combined. Season the mixture and shake in about a tablespoon of Worcester sauce. Clean the frying pan and heat up 1 tablespoon of the oil. Tip the hash into the hot oil and flatten it gently with a slice. Cook for about 5 minutes shaking the pan gently from time to time. When a crust has formed over the bottom of the hash, put a large plate over the pan. Invert the hash on to the plate. Put the last spoonful of oil into the frying pan. Slide the hash back into the pan and cook for a further 5 minutes.

Invert the hash back on to the plate and keep warm in the oven while you poach the eggs. To make perfect poached eggs the eggs need to be as fresh as possible. Fill a heavy-based shallow pan with cold water to a depth of 4 cm/$1^1/_2$ in. Add 2 tablespoons of vinegar. Bring to the boil, then reduce the heat and keep the water just simmering. Break the eggs, one by one, on to a saucer and slide them carefully into the water. Using two spoons, quickly gather the whites over and round the yolks. Cover the pan with a lid and cook the eggs for 4 to 5 minutes, or until the yolk is set and the white is firm.

Serve the hash cut into four large slices, each topped with a poached egg.

# Kromeskis à la Russe

### For the batter

110 g/4 oz/1 cup plain flour

Pinch of salt

1 tablespoon olive oil

150 ml/5 fl oz/½ cup water

1 egg white

### For the Kromeskis

25 g/1 oz /2 tablespoons butter

25 g/1 oz/¼ cup plain flour

150 ml/5 fl oz/½ cup milk

1 egg yolk

Salt and pepper to taste

225 g/8 oz cooked chicken

110 g/4 oz cooked ham

1 tablespoon chopped parsley

1 tablespoon mango chutney

12 cabbage leaves (use a
white cabbage – the leaves
are stronger)

Oil for frying (The amount you
need will depend on the size of
your frying pan or wok. The
Kromeskis need to be covered
with oil while they are cooking.)

Kromeskis à la Russe was served as a supper dish on a West Indian Cruise on the *Laconia* on Monday, 28 January 1929. Kromeskis are a classic dish. They are fiddly but fun. Bear in mind that the chefs had lots of practice and plenty of time. They used the cooked chicken and ham from the luncheon buffet – the Chef de Cuisine had to budget too! The 'à la Russe' means wrapping them in cabbage leaves rather than, as in the original recipe, in bacon.

To make the batter, sift the flour and salt together into a bowl. Make a well in the centre, add the oil and water, and beat until smooth. Allow the mixture to rest for 1 hour while you make the kromeskis.

Melt the butter in a saucepan, stir in the flour and cook the mixture for a few minutes. Then gradually stir in the milk, bring to boil, reduce the heat and simmer for 5 minutes stirring all the time. Take the pan off the heat. Separate the egg, retain the white for use in the batter, and beat the egg yolk into the sauce. Season to taste with pepper and salt. Finely chop the chicken and ham. Add to the sauce with the parsley and chutney. Leave to cool.

Divide the cooled mixture into twelve portions and mould each into a sausage shape on a floured board. Wilt the cabbage in boiling water, just enough so you can mould it. This should only take a minute or so. Wrap each sausage in a cabbage leaf like a little parcel. Leave to set for at least 30 minutes. You can even leave the Kromeskis overnight and finish the dish the next day.

Whisk the egg white until stiff but not dry and stir gently into the batter mixture. Dip each kromeskis in the batter. In a large pan or a wok, fry a few kromeskis at a time in hot deep oil for 5 minutes. Lift out with a slotted spoon and drain on paper towels. Serve hot with either salsa verde or a chilli and tomato relish.

# Le Caneton à L'Orange

Le Caneton à L'Orange or Roast Duck with Orange Sauce was the centrepiece of the huge Menu pour Diner offered to passengers on the *Normandie* on Saturday, 26 December 1936. It was the only item listed in capitals and was qualified as a Specialité Regionale. Duck is a rich, dark meat, full of flavour. The only problem cooks sometimes experience is the amount of fat the bird produces during cooking. Roasting it on a rack solves this. The fresh oranges that garnish the bird and its succulent sauce are satisfyingly tart. All you need in addition is a bowl of perfect steamed new potatoes.

The sauce that accompanies the duck calls for 425 ml/ 15 fl oz/2 cups of duck stock. This must be made in advance, since it needs long slow simmering.

To make the stock, chop the duck giblets and wings into short lengths. Brown them in the oil in a saucepan with the vegetables. Tip out any browning fat. Add the stock, herbs and sufficient water to cover the duck pieces. Simmer the mixture, partially covered, for 1 hour. Strain off the liquid and skim any fat off the top. It is now ready to use.

Preheat the oven to 215°C/425°F/Gas Mark 7. Peel the oranges thinly, taking care not to include the white pith with the thin peel. Cut the peel into short thin strips and simmer in the water in a small pan for 10 minutes. Drain.

Use a third of the drained peel to stuff the body cavity of the bird. Season the cavity and the skin and prick all over with a fork. Roast the bird on a rack in a tin. Start the bird roasting breast down and turn it half way through the cooking time. Reduce the oven temperature after 10 minutes to 180°C/350°F/Gas Mark 4. Roast for approximately 1 hour 15 minutes.

Make the sauce while the duck is roasting. Boil the sugar and red wine vinegar until the mixture has turned into a brown syrup. Stir in the stock gradually. Beat in the arrowroot mixture and stir in the rest of the orange strips. Simmer until the sauce is clear and

4 large oranges

300ml/10 fl oz/1¼ cups water

2kg/4 lb 8 oz duck

Salt and pepper to taste

### For the stock

Duck giblets – neck, liver, gizzard, heart (should be in bag inside the bird when you buy it) plus the wings of the bird

1 tablespoon oil

1 small onion, peeled and sliced

1 medium carrot, peeled and chopped

425 ml/15 fl oz/2 cups vegetable stock

Bay leaf

2 or 3 sprigs of parsley/and or thyme

### For the sauce

3 tablespoons caster sugar

75 ml/2½ fl oz/⅓ cup red wine vinegar

425 ml/15 fl oz/2 cups duck stock

1 level dessertspoon arrowroot or cornflour blended with a little of the duck stock

150 ml/5 fl oz/½ cup port

lightly thickened. Season with salt and pepper to taste. Peel the white pith away from the oranges and cut them into segments.

When the duck is cooked, transfer it to a carving dish and place back in the oven to keep warm. Pour the fat out of the roasting tin. On top of the stove add the port to the tin and boil, scraping vigorously until the liquid is reduced to 3 tablespoons. Add the sauce base and taste, and season with salt and pepper if necessary. Carve the duck and place a few slices on each plate with the orange slices. Reheat the sauce and spoon some over the carved meat.

P&O wine list, c. 1970.

# Coq au Vin Rouge

**This can often be found on the *table d'hote* menus of small restaurants in Burgundy. The chickens raised in the area are particularly tender and the wine, of course, is superb. It was on the Dinner Menu of Union-Castle's *Windsor Castle* steaming between Capetown and Southampton on Wednesday, 17 August 1977.**

Joint the chicken into four large pieces. Melt the butter and olive oil in either a frying pan or a sauté pan just large enough to contain the chicken pieces. Brown the lardons and the onion. Remove with a slice or slotted spoon and set aside while you brown the chicken pieces on all sides until golden brown. Pour the brandy over the chicken and set alight. When the flames die down, pour in just enough red wine to cover the pieces. Add the onion, lardons, garlic, bay leaves and celery. Season carefully with salt and pepper. Cover the pan and simmer for 45 minutes.

Remove the chicken pieces and keep warm in a covered dish. Add the mushrooms to the liquid and simmer for 5 minutes while whisking small pieces of Beurre Manie (see below) into the liquid to thicken the sauce a little. It should be about the consistency of single cream. Cook for a further 5 minutes. Pour the sauce over the chicken pieces, sprinkle with chopped parsley or tarragon and serve. The classic accompaniment to Coq au Vin is Gratin Dauphinois (see page 89) and a green salad on a separate plate.

To make Beurre Manie, use proportions of 1 part flour to 2 parts unsalted butter. Work the butter and flour together until smooth. The easiest way to do this is with a food processor but you can achieve the same result with a fork. Store in the refrigerator covered with cling film.

1 roasting chicken (1.8 kg/4 lb)

50 g/2 oz/4 tablespoons butter

2 tablespoons olive oil

50 g/2 oz lardons /½ cup of bacon

1 medium onion, peeled and finely chopped

1 small glass of brandy, approximately 100 ml/4 fl oz/ ½ cup

Red wine to cover

2 garlic cloves, peeled and chopped

2 bay leaves

1 stick of celery, finely chopped

Salt and pepper to taste

110 g/4 oz small button mushrooms

Chopped parsley or tarragon to garnish

# Salmi of Game

2 young game birds (pheasant, partridge, etc.)

Oil to brush the birds

25 g/1 oz each of onion, carrot and celery, cut into small dice

25 g/1 oz/2 tablespoons butter

1 level dessertspoon flour

425 ml/15 fl oz/2 cups vegetable stock

1 teaspoon tomato purée

1 bay leaf

Sprig of thyme

4 or 5 sprigs of parsley

1 wine glass of red wine

1 wine glass of water

110 g/4 oz button mushrooms

**Young game birds, part roasted, part braised in a rich red wine sauce make up this dish. I found it on the Dinner Menu of the *Lancastria* on Tuesday, 19 February 1929. She was on a West Indies Cruise so I have no idea what game was used. A friend kindly gave me two tender pheasants with which to cook this recipe and joined me for the delicious meal that fed six people. I served the Salmi with redcurrant jelly and purée of celeriac and potato and followed it with a fresh fruit salad.**

Preheat the oven to 180°C/350°F/Gas Mark 4. Brush the birds with oil and set on a trivet in a roasting tin. Roast for 30 minutes. Take out and set aside to cool.

Brown the onion, carrot and celery in the butter. Add the flour and cook for a few minutes more allowing it to brown slowly. Add the stock, tomato purée and herbs, bring to the boil and simmer gently for 20 minutes. Strain through a sieve into a clean saucepan, reserving the vegetables.

Carve the birds and lay the pieces in a casserole. Chop up the carcasses and put them in a saucepan with the glasses of wine and water and the vegetables. Boil rapidly for about 5 minutes then strain back into the sauce. Allow the mixture to simmer for 10 minutes. Pour over the meat, cover the pan and simmer for a further 20 minutes on top of the stove. While the casserole is simmering, wipe the mushrooms clean. Add them to the casserole, put it back in the oven and continue to cook for a further 10 minutes or so. The dish is ready when piping hot.

# 3 HOT VEGETABLES

Hot vegetables were served at every meal including breakfast. On the early menus they don't get much of a mention except as 'vegetables', but by the twentieth century cauliflower, green peas, carrots and green beans begin to make an appearance. Leafing through the huge menus for recent years I lost count of the different vegetables I found.

Occasionally I came across names that sounded very exotic. Succotash is a dish popular in the American south. Fresh corn kernels and broad beans are cooked together, sometimes with green and red peppers, sometimes with butter, sometimes with salt pork. The name was formed from either *misickquatash* or *sukquttahash*, both of which are Narrangansett Indian words. It is a very old recipe; one of the earliest mentions in 1778 refers to corn and beans boiled with bear's flesh. Because of its age and its connection with native America, it is often served at Thanksgiving Dinner and every cook has his or her own version.

We share a language with North America but are also divided by it. Often what started out as exotic turned out to be the American name for very recognizable vegetables. Egg plant is aubergine, zucchini is courgette, Lima beans are broad beans. A few vegetables were more unusual. Oyster plant is salsify, which looks like a long white carrot. On the menu I found it was fried, but it tastes much better steamed or simmered, drained and tossed in butter.

While on the subject of languages, I found that the name of the vegetable dish would often be in English the way it was served in French. Spinach en Branche is leaf spinach, carrots au fines herbes is carrots with chopped fresh herbs, French Beans sauté is French beans tossed in butter.

Occasionally the vegetables served reflected the last port of call. Baked Las Palmas Marrow, Madeira Green Peas and Okra with Tomatoes (served on a West Indian cruise) are some examples.

An oddity is that rice dishes and pasta dishes were often listed under vegetables even if they had a meat or fish sauce. Vegetarian main courses, apart from curry and the occasional vegetarian omelette, do not appear

Passenger List,
SS *Monterey*, 1960,
Matson Lines.

Passenger List

until after 1950 and even then there are not very many of them. As a vegetarian, however, you would not have starved. David Padmore, purser on the Union-Castle Line for many years told me: 'A huge proportion of First-Class passengers didn't choose from the dinner menu but placed individual choices in advance with the Maitre D'.

# Butter Bean, Spinach and Potato Curry

Butter Bean Curry is on the Luncheon Menu for Thursday, 16 April 1936 on P&O's *Moldavia*. The curry recipe listed here is good both as a vegetarian main course or a vegetable accompaniment to a dry Tandoori chicken or lamb dish. It is spicy but mild. You could always add a chopped chilli to the onion if your taste buds prefer. The curry also looks particularly appetising as the spinach stays a beautiful bright green.

On this particular menu every dish had a number, and passengers were requested to order by number. Butter Bean Curry was number 5.

Soak the butter beans for 4 to 5 hours in cold water before starting the recipe.

Drain the butter beans and boil in plenty of water until they are soft. This will take about half an hour. Drain again. If the new potatoes are washed, there is no need to scrape the skins off. Cut them so that they are all approximately the size of a large walnut. Boil or steam them until they are cooked but still firm. Drain and reserve. Wash the spinach.

In a large shallow pan, heat the oil and sauté the onion until it is soft. Add the cumin, coriander, turmeric and fenugreek, stir into the onions and cook gently for a further 5 minutes. Add the coconut milk and let it simmer for 5 minutes. Taste the mixture and add salt if you wish. Add the potatoes, butter beans and the spinach. You will probably have to add the spinach a few leaves at a time. Let them wilt into the curry. Give the whole curry a good stir round and serve with naan bread and mango chutney.

225 g/8 oz/¾ cup butter beans

450 g/1 lb new potatoes

225 g/8 oz fresh spinach

3 tablespoons sunflower or olive oil

1 large onion, peeled and sliced

2 teaspoons ground cumin

2 teaspoons ground coriander

2 teaspoons turmeric

1 teaspoon fenugreek

400 ml/14 fl oz/1¾ cups tinned coconut milk

Salt to taste

# Petits Pois à la Français

225 g/8 oz shallots or pickling onions

2 midget gem lettuces

75 g/3 oz/6 tablespoons butter

150 ml/5 fl oz/⅔ cup water

1 tablespoon caster sugar

675 g/1 lb 8 oz/3 cups fresh or frozen petit pois

Salt and pepper to taste

2 tablespoons chopped parsley

**This is a delectable way to serve peas, so good it could stand on its own as a starter. I found it as one of three vegetables offered on the Dinner Menu on *Normandie* on Saturday, 26 December 1936.**

Peel the shallots and parboil for 10 minutes, then drain. Cut the lettuces into four. Bring the butter, water and sugar to the boil. Add the peas and season with salt and pepper. Add the onions and mix in well. Lay the lettuce quarters on the top of the peas and cover the pan. Bring the peas to the boil and simmer for approximately 10 minutes if they are fresh, 7 minutes if frozen. Turn them several times during the cooking. When they are cooked, there should be very little cooking liquid left. Stir the parsley into the peas, turn everything into a serving dish and serve immediately.

# POTATOES

What can you do with a potato? From the menus I found forty-four different ways of serving them: peeled or not peeled, new or old, boiled, roasted, baked, fried, puréed and sautéed. There were a myriad different names for potato dishes. Some were descriptive; Snow Potatoes are boiled potatoes, put through a potato ricer and served just as they are. However, if you mash the riced potato and start adding other ingredients a variety of names are introduced. Mixed with egg yolk it becomes Duchesse. Formed into rolls, dipped in breadcrumbs and deep-fried the Duchesse potatoes become Croquettes. The Croquettes rolled in almonds become Almondines; with added truffles they are Pommes Berny.

Some names refer to the shape carved by the chef; Pont-Neuf, Château, Fondant are all oval shapes. Straw, Mignonettes, Allumettes or Matchstick and French Fries are all sizes of oblong chip. Maxim, Rissolé and Parmentier are small to large potato dice. Judging by the number of times these names came up, there must have been a young chef carving away every day in most galleys.

From such interesting names as Saratoga Potatoes, Potatoes O'Brien, Garfield Potatoes, Pommes Bataille, Pommes Château, Pommes Cocotte and Pommes Voisin, which recipe should I choose to represent the daily potato dishes?

In the end I opted for two favourites, one from the Old World – Gratin Dauphinois, which is scalloped potatoes baked in the oven in a mixture of cream and butter and just a hint of garlic, and one from the New World – Hashed Brown Potatoes, a favourite in any American diner.

Simple mashed potato is offered on the Children's Menu, *Aureol*, 1953, Elder Dempster Line.

# Gratin Dauphinois

900 g/2 lb large potatoes

400 ml/14 fl oz/1¾ cups single cream

1 garlic clove

50 g/2 oz/4 tablespoons butter

Salt and pepper to taste

Grated nutmeg to taste

**Gratin Dauphinois was on the Dinner Menu on the *Parthia* on 3 January 1958. She was on a week's voyage and served no less than twenty-one different potato dishes during the seven days – a heroic effort of planning by the chef.**

Preheat the oven to 170°C/325°F/Gas Mark 3. Peel and slice the potatoes very thinly. Heat the cream in a saucepan large enough to hold the potatoes as well. Bring to the boil and add the potatoes. Simmer for 5 minutes while you prepare the gratin dish. Cut the garlic clove in half and rub the inside of the dish with it. Then butter the dish generously. Put half the potato mixture in the dish, season with salt and pepper and grated nutmeg, and cover with the second half. Smooth the top and dot with the remaining butter. Season with more salt and pepper. Bake for approximately 1 hour. The top should be golden brown and the potato slices soft and cooked. This is a perfect accompaniment to grilled steak or roast lamb.

# Hashed Brown Potatoes

**This recipe formed part of a Luncheon Menu on the *Queen Elizabeth* as she steamed between Southampton and New York on Saturday, 13 April 1958. It was also found on Breakfast Menus where it constituted a 'home from home' dish for Americans.**

675 g/1 lb 8 oz potatoes, peeled and cut into quarters

110 g/4 oz streaky bacon

25 g/1 oz/2 tablespoons butter

Salt and pepper to taste

Put the potatoes in a large saucepan, cover with cold water, bring to the boil and cook until they are tender. Drain in a colander. Leave to cool then cut them into small dice. Cook the bacon in a frying pan, preferably non-stick, until it has rendered all its fat and is crisp and brown. Remove with a slice and drain on paper towels. Add the butter to the bacon fat and melt. Put in the diced potato, season to taste with salt and pepper, then press them down firmly into the pan with a slice. The potatoes should form a pancake about 5 cm/2 in. thick. Cook over a moderate heat, shaking the pan occasionally to stop the potatoes sticking. A golden brown crust should form on the bottom surface in about 15 to 20 minutes.

To serve, cover the pan with a heated plate or shallow dish and invert. Crumble the reserved crisp bacon over the top and serve immediately.

# THE COLD TABLE

The Cold Table, The Cold Buffet, Le Buffet Froid is on nearly every Luncheon and Dinner Menu from the earliest to the latest that I looked at. Cold dishes were available on every menu including Breakfast.

Sometimes The Cold Table was set up to the side of the dining saloon. A sumptuous banquet would be laid out. Dishes such as Poached Salmon Decorated with Cucumber and Hollandaise Sauce, Roast Sirloin of Beef with Horseradish Cream, Roast Duckling with Apple Sauce, Roast Quarters of Lamb with Mint Sauce, Baked Cumberland Ham, Roast Turkey with Cranberry Sauce, Galantine of Veal, and a pie – Windsor, Leicester or Melton Mowbray – would be displayed alongside various salads with their appropriate dressings. The chef would be waiting behind the table, hat on head, carving knife and fork in hand to cut the choicest slices. Passengers also remember with affection, on cruises or more leisurely passages, spectacular buffets on deck, with prawns in the shell and lobsters lending a shell fish aspect to the display.

There are a couple of showy dishes in this chapter. Jambon de York Decoré or Decorated York Ham is a whole ham, poached in cider then glazed with brown sugar and Dijon mustard, and studded with cloves. It looks magnificent and tastes even better.

A joint of ham was a great favourite on the menus. Sometimes simply described as 'Cold Ham', it is often qualified with the region of origin as above. The *Normandie* had hams from Virginia, Prague, Westphalia and Bayonne as well as York on the same menu.

Beef Wellington was named after the Duke of Wellington, the great soldier and victor of the Battle of Waterloo. The fillet of beef is sealed, moistened with buttered, 'herby', chopped mushrooms and encased in puff pastry. Bake the pastry and you have a great golden parcel, which looks wonderful whole or sliced. It tastes good hot as well.

There are many, many mentions of galantines. A galantine can be either a bird or a joint of meat 'boned, cooked, pressed and served cold with aspic'. I have chosen a recipe for its cousin, a terrine – a layered loaf or paté served cold. Mousses of meat, fish and chicken also abound, you will find a Mousse of Chicken au Paprika.

Accompanying these main dishes were all kinds of salads. Some need no introduction; green, tomato, cucumber, potato and beetroot are simple. Some are incredibly elaborate. I came across Bagration on a menu from HMT *Strathmore*, carrying troops during the Second World War. It was made up of 'Julienne of celery and chicken and artichoke bottoms, macaroni and tomatoes, decorated with truffles, eggs, chopped parsley and mayonnaise sauce'. The French chef, Antonin Carème, invented it for and named it after Pierre, Prince Bagration, a Russian general who was killed at the Battle of Borodino. He must have been an appreciative gourmet; there is also a Sole Bagration and two Soups Bagration on the menus.

The names were fascinating, I tracked down the ingredients of Salade Yam Yam, which was 'French beans, slices of cucumbers, julienne of celeriac, quarters of lettuces, vinaigrette', but I haven't managed to find those for Salad Palm Beach or Salad Bath and Tennis Club, both served on a Mediterranean cruise on the *Queen Mary* in 1966. Operas inspire salads: Salad Manon, on many menus including the *Laconia* on a Cunard West Indies Cruise in 1929, is much simpler, but still a combination we might not often find today. 'Lettuces, quarters of grapefruit, lemon juice, pepper from the mill and vinaigrette'.

The salad recipes I have chosen might well have appeared as starters on a trolley. I found that people talked with much affection about the hors d'oeuvres trolley. Most of them had been children when they had travelled as passengers on the liners in the 1950s and 1960s. Great Britain was just emerging from wartime and the rigours of rationing, and the sight of a trolley laden with cold meats, fishes and salads, from which you could choose as much as you liked, must have seemed impossibly luxurious to young eyes.

The restaurant staff on the
*Windsor Castle*, c. 1960,
Union-Castle.

# Beef Wellington

Beef Wellington is classic luxury food. It was part of The Cold Table buffet on the *Windsor Castle* on Friday, 2 September 1977. Its French name is Boeuf en Croûte. It looks spectacular and tastes just as good, so it is the perfect dish for maximum display and then good eating. Consisting of fillet of beef, surrounded by a rich farce or stuffing, then baked in a pastry case, the meat is rare when sliced.

Recipes differ on the ingredients for the stuffing round the meat. Classic French recipes suggest foie gras. My version suggests sautéed mushrooms flavoured with garlic and lemon.

Preheat the oven to 190°C/375°F/Gas Mark 5. Trim any fat off the fillet and tie it into a neat sausage with rounds of string at intervals. If it tapers off at either end, tuck the end under and tie it in so that the sausage is an even thickness throughout. Brush the fillet with olive oil. Heat a non-stick saucepan until good and hot and fry the fillet quickly until it is brown on all sides. The meat should be sealed and firm.

Chop the mushrooms very small either by hand or in a food processor. Melt the butter in a frying pan and fry the mushrooms, garlic and the lemon zest together until soft. Leave to cool.

Roll out the pastry to an oblong, large enough to take the sides up and seal them over the top of the joint and long enough to seal the ends well. Set the beef on the pastry and remove the strings. Turn the mushroom mixture into a sieve to remove as much moisture as possible, then cover the joint with the mushroom and garlic mix. Bring the two sides of the pastry up to join above the meat. Using a pastry brush seal the join above and at either end of the meat with the egg and milk. Pinch the join between two fingers and nick it with scissors at 5 cm/1$^1$/$_2$ in. intervals and turn each piece alternate directions to seal and decorate the top. This also allows air holes for steam to escape when the case is cooking.

1.3 kg/3 lb fillet of beef

1 tablespoon olive oil

450 g/1 lb mushrooms

25 g/2 tablespoons unsalted butter

2 garlic cloves, chopped

Grated zest of half a lemon

450 g/1 lb ready-made puff pastry

1 egg yolk mixed with 75 ml/ 3 fl oz/$^1$/$_3$ cup milk

Parsley to garnish

Check that you have encased the meat completely at either end and brush the case with the remaining egg and milk mixture.

Set on a roasting tin lined with baking parchment and bake in the hot oven for 25 minutes. The pastry should be golden brown. The meat will still be pink inside.

Let the case cool on the baking parchment. This should make it easy to move to a serving dish. Garnish with parsley. Serve cut into thick slices. Horseradish sauce or mustard are classic accompaniments.

'Gibraltar', by Charles Pears, 1928.

# Jambon de York Decoré

**Otherwise known as York Ham, Baked Ham and Cold Ham, it appeared under the French title above on the Luncheon Menu at the launch of the *Lusitania* on 7 June 1906. Below is a good method of cooking any sized joint of ham, from the smallest rolled piece to the largest piece on the bone. It also leaves you with some wonderful stock to use in soups or sauces.**

Weigh the gammon and calculate the simmering time. You should allow approximately 15 minutes per 450 g/1 lb. Put the gammon in a large saucepan and tip in the cider, then fill the pot with water so that the gammon is submerged. Peel and chop the carrot and onion, chop the celery and add to the pot with the peppercorns. Bring to the boil, cover the pan with a lid or foil, then turn the heat down and simmer for the allotted time. While the joint is simmering, preheat the oven to 200°C/400°F/Gas Mark 6.

Lift the joint from the pot (retain the cooking stock for another recipe). Allow it to cool slightly, then peel off the skin. Score a diamond pattern in the fat with a sharp knife. Mix the brown sugar with the mustard until you have a smooth paste and smear this on the top of the joint. Then stud the diamond intersections with cloves. Set the ham on a baking tin lined with baking parchment and roast for 30 minutes.

Joint of gammon (this can be boned and rolled or on the bone)

Mixture of water and cider sufficient to cover the joint in the proportion two-thirds water to one-third cider

1 carrot

1 small onion

1 stick of celery

½ teaspoon black peppercorns

### For the glaze

4 tablespoons soft brown sugar

2 tablespoons Dijon mustard

Dried cloves

## MENU.

Mayonnaise de Saumon Froid, Salade de Concombres.

Paupiettes de Sole à la Princesse.

Aspic de Crevettes à la Victoria.

Cailles en Caisse.      Soufflé de Volaille à la Marie Louise.

Aspic de Foie Gras aux Truffles,      Chaudfroid de Côtelettes d'Agneau.

Pâté de Pigeon Bordeaux.

Hure de Sanglier à la St. Hubert.

Quartiers d'Agneau Rôti, Sauce Menthe.      Bœuf Braise à la Benoist.

Aloyau de Bœuf Rôti.      Dinde Rôtis aux Cresson.

Galantine de Capon aux Pistaches.      Langue de Bœuf à l'Ecarlate.

Jambon de York Decoré.

Salade de Homard.      Salade de Tomate.

Trifle à l'Ecossaise.      Meringue Monté aux Apricot.

Baba au Rhum.      Charlotte Russe au Chocolat.

Crème à la Duchesse.      Gelées Variées.

Gâteau Breton.

Fraises à la Crème.

Fruits.      Glacés Variée.

Bonbons.

Caramels.      Petits Fours.

Café Noir.

LUNCHEON
on the occasion
of the **LAUNCH** of the
CUNARD
TURBINE STEAMER
"Lusitania"
at
John Brown & Coy., Ltd's
SHEFFIELD
AND
CLYDEBANK.

Luncheon Menu on the launch of the
*Lusitania*, 1906, Cunard.

# Pork Terrine with Chicken

Terrines or galantines were perennial favourites. I found a Terrine of Duckling on a Dinner Menu on the *Queen Mary* on 3 March 1966 and a Galantine of Fowl on the Luncheon Menu on the *Titanic* on 14 April 1912, the day before the disaster. I have chosen a French classic terrine recipe. Unmoulded it is beautiful, decorated with fresh bay leaves. When sliced, each slice is studded with chicken breast. It can be served as a lunch dish, as part of a buffet, or for hearty appetites as a first course.

Preheat the oven to 175°C/350°F/Gas Mark 4. Lay the bay leaves, shiny side down, in the bottom of a 900 g/2 lb loaf tin in a fan shape. Then line the tin, over the bay leaves, with streaky bacon rashers.

Mix the filling as follows. Melt the butter in a small pan and fry the onion until soft. Leave it to cool. If you have a food processor, chop the belly of pork into cubes and process into coarse mince. (If you have no processor, ask the butcher to do this for you when you buy the pork). Chop the chicken livers into small pieces.

Put the cooled onion, the pork mince, chicken livers, garlic, allspice, cloves, nutmeg, beaten egg and brandy into a large bowl. Season with the salt and pepper. Beat with a wooden spoon to combine. It should be quite a wet mixture.

Spread one-third of the mixture in the tin, cover with a layer of chicken strips. Repeat the process ending with a layer of stuffing. Cover the tin with a layer of greaseproof paper, then a layer of foil and see that it is well tucked round the tin. Place in a roasting tin. Fill the roasting tin with hot water to come half way up the loaf tin. Bake for $1^1/_2$ hours. The water should simmer during this time. If too much evaporates, add more.

---

3 bay leaves

225 g/8 oz streaky bacon, rindless

15 g/½ oz/1 tablespoon butter

1 medium onion, peeled and finely chopped

675 g/1 lb 8 oz belly of pork, about half fat, half lean meat

225 g/8 oz chicken livers

2 garlic cloves, peeled and finely chopped

½ teaspoon allspice

Pinch of ground cloves

Pinch of ground nutmeg

2 eggs, beaten

2 tablespoons brandy

1 teaspoon salt

Freshly ground pepper

1 large or 2 small chicken breasts, cut into strips

---

Allow to cool. Press the terrine to firm it up if you can by putting a large weight on the top when it is cold. Refrigerate for three days if possible to increase the flavour. To serve, run a knife round the edge of the terrine and turn out onto an oval plate. Slice thickly; the terrine should be marbled with pale chicken chunks. Serve with rough slices of good bread, a green salad and either chutney or the classic accompaniment of pickled gherkins.

Dining salon, *Aquitania*, 1914, Cunard.

# Mousse of Chicken au Paprika

**Mousses, galantines, terrines of chicken and duck are the traditional staples of The Cold Table. Galleys would have had plentiful supplies of cold fowls and stock, the basic ingredients of these dishes. Galantine of Fowl was on the Luncheon Menu of the *Titanic* on 14 April 1912 and Galantine of Capon on a menu of the *Viceroy of India* in 1935. Galantines are a mousse encased in a boned and stuffed bird and poached in a cloth in stock. This is quite difficult to achieve in a domestic kitchen; so I have chosen a mousse served on the *Himalaya* as part of the dinner buffet on Sunday, 27 November 1949.**

Melt the butter and sauté the chicken livers for 5 minutes. Set aside to cool.

Take out a little of the stock in a cup. Sprinkle the gelatine on the top and stir to make a purée. Heat the stock and paprika to just below boiling and stir in the gelatine through a sieve (a tea strainer works well). You are less likely to find lumps this way. If you find it is not blending evenly give the mixture a whisk. Stir and let it cool a little. Put the chicken, livers, stock mixture and herbs in a food processor. Process until you have the texture you want. Tip the contents into a mixing bowl and stir in the sherry or brandy. Season with salt and pepper and Tabasco or chilli sauce. You may want to slightly over-season, as the cream that goes in next will make the mixture blander.

Whip the cream softly. Fold it into the mixture and adjust the seasoning. Oil a 1.5 litre/3 pint/6 cup mould. Place the mixture inside and smooth the top. Chill, covered in the refrigerator, for several hours before un-moulding.

30 g/1 oz/2 tablespoons butter

110 g/4 oz chicken livers

425 ml/15 fl oz/scant 2 cups chicken stock

30 g/1 oz/¼ cup gelatine (comes in 30 g/1 oz packs, so 1 pack)

1 level teaspoon paprika

450 g/1 lb cooked, chopped chicken

3 tablespoons chopped fresh herbs, any mixture of chives and tarragon and parsley

2 tablespoons sherry or brandy

Salt and Pepper to taste

Few drops of Tabasco or chilli sauce

150 ml/5 fl oz/½ cup double cream

# Oignons à la Grecque

450 g/1 lb small 'pickling' onions

425 ml/15 fl oz/scant 2 cups water

150 ml/5 fl oz/½ cup extra virgin olive oil

150 ml/5 fl oz/$^1$/$_2$ cup lemon juice

½ teaspoon salt

12 peppercorns

12 coriander seeds

2 finely chopped shallots

1 tablespoon finely chopped celery

1 dessertspoon chopped parsley

1 dessertspoon chopped fennel

Sprig of fresh thyme

3 tablespoons chopped parsley or mixed green herbs to garnish

**I found this aromatic 'cooked' salad on a Dinner Menu from the *Queen Mary* on Thursday, 3 March 1966, when she was on a Mediterranean cruise. Despite the name, this is a French recipe and variations appear in all classic French cook books.**

Drop the onions for 1 minute into boiling water. Drain and peel them, then cut a cross in their root ends so that they cook evenly. Place all the other ingredients except the garnish into a saucepan large enough to take the onions as well as the liquid and simmer for 10 minutes. Add the onions to the vegetable broth and simmer until they are tender. They will probably take between 30 and 40 minutes.

Remove the onions with a slotted spoon and put them in a serving dish. Boil down the liquid for 5 minutes and season with more salt and pepper if you wish. Pour over the onions. Allow them to cool and sprinkle over the parsley or mixed herbs before serving. The onions are delicious served either at room temperature or chilled.

# Pickled Fish/Gravadlax

**I found Pickled Fish on the First Class Luncheon Menu on the *Windsor Castle* on Friday, 2 September 1977 travelling between Capetown and Southampton. Does it sound more elegant under its other name 'Gravadlax'? No matter, the result is the same. Originally from Scandinavia, the recipe is simplicity itself, although you do have to start some days before you need to serve the tender slices of salmon, flavoured just a little with dill and mustard. A squeeze of lemon and the Pickled Fish or Gravadlax is ready.**

Ask the fishmonger for a cut from the thick end of the fillet, and allow approximately 50 g/2 oz of salmon per serving. Start this dish at least three days before you wish to serve it.

Cut a piece of cling film large enough to wrap the salmon. Scatter rock salt on the cling film. Spread both sides of the salmon, first with the mustard, then with the dill, to cover the fish completely. Wrap the salmon in the cling film, place on a dish and chill for at least three days, turning from time to time. It is not necessary to unwrap the fish when you turn it.

To serve, unwrap the cling film, slice the salmon thinly, garnish with lemon wedges and serve with brown bread and butter, a little green frisée and a dill sauce or mayonnaise.

450 g/1 lb fresh salmon fillet, skinned

Coarsely ground rock salt

Coarse grain mustard

1 packet fresh dill (you can use dried dill if fresh is not available), finely chopped

Freshly ground pepper

Lemon wedges to garnish

# Potted Fish

2 tablespoons medium dry white wine

Juice and grated zest of 1 lemon (retain 1 teaspoon of the zest to use in the clarified butter)

150 g/6 oz/10 tablespoons soft butter

225 g/8 oz flaked cooked salmon

Salt, pepper and freshly grated nutmeg to taste

**For the lemon clarified butter**

50 g/2 oz/4 tablespoons butter

2 tablespoons water

'Potting' has been used for several hundred years as a way to preserve fish or meat. I have chosen salmon as the fish, because the richness of this and the butter contrasts so well with the lemon juice. It makes a good first course or a light meal served with a salad. Potted Fish was on several menus I looked at, including the Luncheon Menu of the *Viceroy of India* on Wednesday, 26 June 1935.

Bring the wine, lemon zest, and juice to the boil and boil hard until reduced to 1 tablespoonful of liquid. Remove from the heat and beat with softened butter until creamy. Combine with the flaked salmon and season to taste with the salt, pepper and nutmeg. Mix well and spoon into four small ramekins. Seal with the lemon clarified butter.

To make the lemon clarified butter, bring the teaspoon of lemon zest, butter and water slowly to the boil. Remove from the heat, allow to cool slightly and gently spoon over the potted fish.

Chill the ramekins in the refrigerator for at least a couple of hours. Serve with hot toast or Melba toast. Potted salmon keeps well in the fridge for two or three days.

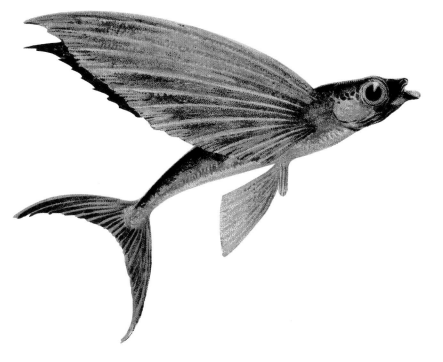

# Tomatoes Ravigote

**Tomatoes Ravigote was on the Dinner Menu of the *Saxonia* on Tuesday, 29 August 1961. This is a classic French sauce using vinaigrette and appears on other menus accompanying cold meats. The marriage of the fresh, sharp tastes in the Ravigote and ripe, sweet tomatoes works particularly well.**

Whisk the wine vinegar, oil, sugar, salt, mustard and pepper together until well blended. Stir in the capers, shallots and fresh herbs. Slice the tomatoes on to a large shallow dish. Pour over the dressing. Serve as part of a cold meal.

1 tablespoon white wine vinegar

6 tablespoons extra virgin olive oil

1 teaspoon sugar

½ teaspoon salt

1 teaspoon Dijon mustard

Freshly ground black pepper

1 teaspoon chopped capers

1 teaspoon very finely chopped shallots or spring onions

2 tablespoons chopped fresh herbs (parsley, tarragon and chives, or parsley only)

1 large firm tomato per person

# Salade Russe

2 medium carrots

1 medium turnip

175 g/6 oz cauliflower

175 g/6 oz celeriac

175 g/6 oz green beans

175 g/6 oz/1 cup frozen petit pois

4 tablespoons vinaigrette (see page 106)

25 ml/4 fl oz/½ cup mayonnaise (see page 107)

2 tablespoons finely chopped mixed fresh green herbs, chives, parsley and tarragon, on their own or any combination.

Salade Russe or Russian Salad is a salad of just-cooked vegetables dressed while warm with vinaigrette and then when cooled with mayonnaise and herbs. Freshly made it is both lovely to look at and good to eat. From a tin it is quite a different dish.

It was on the Luncheon Menu of the *Saxonia* on Tuesday, 29 August 1961. The chef on the *Saxonia* made it clear on the menu that he was confident he could cook any dish for any client from anywhere in the world. I would have loved to have tasted his Salade Russe to see which vegetables he thought appropriate. Below is my choice but do experiment.

Peel the carrots and turnip and cut into batons. Separate the cauliflower into florets. Peel the celeriac and cut into dice. The best way to cook these vegetables, plus the green beans, is to steam them. They need approximately 5 minutes each. The vegetables should be cooked but crunchy. If you do not have a steamer, they can be simmered in boiling salted water for 5 minutes and drained. Cook the petit pois for 3 minutes in boiling salted water and drain. Mix the vegetables while still warm with the vinaigrette, turning them well to absorb the dressing. Let them cool then mix in the mayonnaise and one tablespoon of fresh herbs. Turn into a bowl and use the second tablespoon of herbs to garnish the dish.

# SALAD DRESSINGS

I found over twenty named dressings on the Luncheon and Dinner menus. Vinaigrette, or French dressing, is usually on the list. Mayonnaise, too, is often there. Others such as Roquefort, 'crumbled Roquefort cheese with vinaigrette or sour cream', Russian, 'vinaigrette or mayonnaise with chilli sauce and diced red or green pepper', Vert, 'very finely chopped watercress and parsley with mayonnaise' were names that
I recognized. Mignonette, St Louis, Rabelais, Chantilly were names I did not. Once I had started researching the recipes
I found all these exotic dressings are variations, with additions of herbs, spices, chopped vegetables, cream, or essences, to either Vinaigrette or Mayonnaise. So those are the recipes I have provided in this section. They are both emulsions, the first oil and vinegar or lemon, the second, eggs, oil and vinegar or lemon. Additionally I have included a recipe for Thousand Islands dressing. This, too, appeared on a number of menus. Like mayonnaise and vinaigrette, there are many recipes for it.

# Vinaigrette/French Dressing

**This will make approximately 150 ml/5 fl oz/$^1/_2$ cup (enough to dress two mixed salads for four people)**

Mix the wine vinegar, salt, sugar and mustard together and season with black pepper. Whisk in the oil slowly. If the dressing is going to stand for some time before you use it, you will need to whisk again before you dress the salad. Vinaigrette is intensely personal. Every cook has different proportions. The mustard and sugar are optional. I like them. Leave them out if you do not. Reduce or increase the vinegar to your taste.

2 tablespoons wine vinegar

Pinch of salt

Pinch of sugar

1 teaspoon Dijon mustard

Freshly ground pepper

6 tablespoons olive oil

# Mayonnaise

1 egg

1 tablespoon lemon juice or wine vinegar

1 teaspoon Dijon mustard

Pinch of salt

Freshly ground black pepper

300 ml/10 fl oz/1¼ cups olive oil

This will make approximately 425 ml/15 fl oz/nearly 2 cups. Making mayonnaise by hand can be tricky but this recipe, devised to be made in a food processor or blender, is much easier. It usually helps to have all the ingredients at room temperature before you start.

Break the egg into the food processor or blender. Blend for 30 seconds. Add the lemon juice or wine vinegar, mustard, a pinch of salt, some freshly ground pepper and start to process. Add the oil drop by drop; you will have a thick creamy mixture in seconds. This will keep for about 5 days in a refrigerator.

# Thousand Islands

150 ml/5 fl oz/½ cup mayonnaise

1 tablespoon pimento stuffed green olives, finely chopped

1 teaspoon chopped shallots

1 hardboiled egg, finely chopped

1 teaspoon capers

1 teaspoon tomato purée

2 teaspoons chopped chives

Few drops of chilli sauce

May Irwin, a leading American actress in the early twentieth century, is credited with christening this mixture of tomato-flavoured mayonnaise with added pickles, herbs and chopped hardboiled egg, after the Thousand Islands on the St Lawrence River in upstate New York. It was invented by her friend Sophia Lalonde, wife of a fishing guide on the river. Irwin gave the recipe to the owner of the Waldorf Astoria Hotel in New York and the rest, of course, is history.

Recipes for the dressing vary wildly; the one I have chosen involves all the ingredients originally listed.

Make the mayonnaise as in the previous recipe. Mix in all the rest of the ingredients.

# 5 PUDDINGS

In the lavish world of the great liners, the pudding course was an excuse for the chef to really show off. In the 1920s and 1930s, this meant a hot sweet soufflé. A soufflé needs even heat in the oven, a strong hand with the whisk, iron nerves and split-second timing. Soufflés won't wait. I have included the delicious Soufflé Rothschild, but make it for friends who don't mind being organized.

Every ship carried a pâtissier, a pastry cook who would put together spectacular gateaux – triple layered cakes, stuffed with cream and fruit and elaborately decorated. I found over a dozen different gateaux and chose an old favourite from the post-war era – Black Forest Gateau.

Ice creams are on every menu. They must have been very welcome on the trips to the East and the southern hemisphere in the days before air conditioning. Some were deliciously fruity, probably using the fresh fruits loaded on at the last port of call. Many were the classics we all know. I have included a recipe for Vanilla Ice Cream, which can also be served as an alternative to cream or custard for many puddings. It is an integral element of Peach Melba, which is also here. Although Peach Melba is more 'combining' than cooking, it is on many menus. It is so delicious and the story behind the dish is so delightful, I had to include it.

Coupes are particular combinations of fruit, sweet sauces and ice cream. The word *coupe* is French for bowl. There were many different Coupes. Coupe Bienvenue was served on the first evening of a trip and Coupe Au Revoir on the last. I was intrigued by a Coupe Edna May, which I found on several menus. Who was Edna May and what was her Coupe? A beautiful musical actress, the toast of New York and London before 1914, and vanilla ice cream with hot brandied black cherry sauce, were the answers.

Steamed puddings were always popular. I have included a Pouding aux Prunes Anglais, better known to us as Christmas Pudding. You will see that although Plum Pudding is on every Christmas Day Menu, it was also served on other occasions. It was difficult to choose another representative. Black Cap Pudding won because I loved the contrast between the blackcurrant topping and the lemony pudding.

Rhubarb and Apple Charlotte, Gooseberry and Ginger Pie and

Menu covers on the *Iberia* decorated with the exotic fruits Carambola (left) and Custard Apple (right), 1962, P&O.

Compote of Plums are all stalwarts of English cooking and I have included a recipe for custard. If you have never made a crème pâtissière/custard before, you are in for a fantastic surprise. It is delectable, hot or cold. It, too, is the basis of other recipes, including one of the highlights of English cuisine I could not leave out. A well-made trifle is the perfect combination of flavours and textures.

Whilst on the subject of English cuisine, there were many milk puddings on the menus from the first to the last; Tapioca Custard, Semolina Pudding, Sago Pudding, Vermicelli Custard and Blancmange all are there. I have to admit to subjectivity. The last time I ate these puddings was as a child and I didn't like them. Rice pudding I did like, so Rice and Raisin Pudding represents them.

Port Wine Jelly or Wine Jelly is a grown-up version of a childhood favourite. Both puddings feature across the years. I have combined the two and given a recipe for Port and Claret Jelly.

If you want to spoil yourself and your friends or family and spend a little time doing it, then you are going to enjoy these recipes. A good pudding can make an enjoyable meal really memorable.

# Black Forest Gateaux/Schwarzwalder Kirschtorte

This sumptuous cake has suffered from rather bad press. In its heyday of the 1970s, inferior restaurants bought in inferior versions. Since the galley had a pâtissier, I am sure it was freshly made when I found it on the Dinner Menu of the *Windsor Castle* for Wednesday, 17 August 1977. Made carefully at home, it can be a showy, delicious treat. It does need time; start cooking well ahead of the party.

To make the chocolate curls, make sure the chocolate is straight out of the refrigerator. Hold the chocolate over a shallow tin lined with foil and shave the block with a vegetable peeler. Make a selection of thick and thin curls. Handle the chocolate as little as possible. Cover the curls loosely with foil and refrigerate until you need them.

To make the cake: preheat the oven to 175°C/350°F/Gas Mark 4. Butter and dust with flour the insides of three round 18 cm/7 in. cake tins. Cut a piece of baking parchment to fit the bottom of each tin.

Clarify the butter by melting it in a small saucepan very slowly over a low heat. Do not let it brown. Let it rest for a minute or two then spoon the clear butter into a bowl and throw away the milky residue at the bottom of the pan.

Beat the eggs, vanilla extract and sugar together with an electric whisk until the mixture is light, pale and fluffy. Sift the flour and the cocoa over the egg mixture a little at a time folding it in very gently with a large metal spoon or a rubber spatula. Finally add the clarified butter 2 tablespoons at a time. Do not overmix. Gently pour the batter into the prepared cake tins, dividing it equally among all three. Bake the cakes in the centre of the oven for about 15 minutes. Test by inserting a metal skewer into the centre of each cake. The cake is ready when the skewer comes out clean. Remove from the oven. Let them cool in the tins for about 5 minutes. Then run a sharp knife round the edge of each cake and turn them out on wire racks to cool completely. Peel the paper off the bottom of each cake.

For the chocolate curls

225 g/8 oz plain chocolate

For the cake

150 g/5 oz/10 tablespoons unsalted butter

6 eggs (at room temperature)

1/2 teaspoon vanilla extract

225 g/8 oz/1 cup caster sugar

50 g/2 oz/½ cup flour

50 g/2oz/2 tablespoons cocoa

For the syrup

75 g/3 oz sugar

200 ml/7 fl oz/scant 1 cup water

4 tablespoons Kirsch (brandy is not so authentic but also tastes good)

For the filling and topping

700 ml/1¼ pints/3 cups double cream

50 g/2 oz/½ cup icing sugar

175 g/6 oz tinned stoned black cherries, drained of their syrup and dried on paper towels

While you are waiting for the cakes to cool, make the syrup. Put the sugar and water into a small saucepan and bring to the boil stirring until the sugar dissolves. Boil briskly, uncovered, for 5 minutes. Remove from the heat, leave to cool until lukewarm and stir in the kirsch.

Transfer the cooled cakes to baking parchment and prick well with a carving fork. Sprinkle the cakes evenly with the syrup and let them rest for 5 minutes.

Next make the filling and topping. Whisk the cream until it thickens a little. Sift the icing sugar over the cream and continue whisking until the cream forms firm peaks.

To assemble the gateau, place one of the cakes on a serving plate. Spread the top with a 1½ cm/½ in. layer of whipped cream. Strew one third of the cherries over the top. Gently set another cake on the top and repeat the process. Set the third cake in place. Spread the sides and the top of the cake with the rest of the cream. Decorate the top with the final third of cherries. Gently press the chocolate curls on the side of the cake and arrange them on the top over the cream and cherries. Chill until required.

*Shakespeare's A Midsummer Night's Dream inspired this Union-Castle Menu.*

# Almond Slices

**These were served on the *Strathmore* as a dessert at dinner on Thursday, 22 January 1938. I have no indication of the exact recipe and almond slices are often made without fruit, but I think the crunchy texture of the pear and the sharpness of the lemon are a winning combination.**

Preheat the oven to 200°C/450°F/Gas Mark 8. Cut the pastry into two pieces and roll out two oblongs, approximately 28 cm x 21.5 cm/11 in. x 9 in. Cut each into six oblong pieces. Lay six of these pieces on a metal baking sheet lined with baking parchment and prick all over with a fork. Mix the ground almonds, icing sugar and lemon juice together until smooth. Divide the mixture into six and spread it on each piece of pastry leaving a small margin round the edges. Peel and core the pears, cut each in half, slice the halves and arrange the slices on top of the ground almond mixture. Brush the edges of the pastry with milk and lay one of the remaining pastry oblongs on top of each. Bake for approximately 20 minutes or until well risen and brown.

Take out of the oven and allow to cool. When the slices are room temperature, mix the icing sugar with the lemon juice for the glacé and use at once to coat the tops. Sprinkle a few toasted almonds over each before the icing sets. Serve at room temperature with pouring cream or crème fraîche.

450 g/1 lb ready-made puff pastry

175 g/6 oz/½ cups ground almonds

175 g/6 oz/1½ cups icing sugar

Juice of 1 lemon

2 ripe pears

Little milk for brushing

Handful of toasted flaked almonds

### For the glacé icing

100 g/4 oz/¾ cup icing sugar

1 tablespoon of lemon juice.

# Black Cap Pudding

110 g/4 oz/8 tablespoons unsalted butter

110 g/4 oz/½ cup caster sugar

2 eggs

50 g/2 oz/½ cup self-raising flour

50 g/2 oz/1 cup fresh white breadcrumbs

Grated zest of 1 lemon

1 to 2 tablespoons Madeira or medium sherry

3 tablespoons blackcurrant jam

**This was served at dinner on a Las Palmas Cruise on the *Queen Mary* on Saturday, 25 March 1967. The British are famous for their steamed puddings. This is particularly light and lemony. Topping it with blackcurrant jam is inspired and, of course, the colour contrasts are wonderful.**

Butter a 1.5 litre/2 pint/4½ cup pudding basin. Cream the butter and sugar together until pale and fluffy. Whisk the eggs, then add them a little at a time to the butter and sugar, beating well between each addition. Sieve the flour and fold in gently. Stir in the breadcrumbs and lemon zest together with the Madeira or sherry. Put the blackcurrant jam in the bottom of the buttered basin. Spoon the mixture over the top. Cover first with greaseproof paper. Put a pleat in the greaseproof, so the pudding has room to rise when it is cooked. Cover this loosely with foil and tie the lid down with string. Steam for 2 to 2½ hours or until well risen. If you are steaming in a saucepan, stand the bowl on an upturned saucer and fill the pan with boiling water; the water should come about half way up the basin. Top up with more water as necessary.

To serve, turn the pudding out on a warm dish. Serve hot or warm with pouring cream.

# Compote of Plums and Custard

**This was offered as a pudding on the *Queen Elizabeth* on Saturday, 9 November 1963. Does it sound more exciting in French – Compote de Prunes avec Crème Anglaise? Language aside, it is the most delicious combination and the perfect finish to a rich meal.**

Halve the plums and remove the stones. Put a shallow pan – a frying pan with a lid is ideal – on the heat and dissolve the sugar and lemon juice in the water, stirring to stop the sugar catching. When it has dissolved, add the cinnamon stick broken up into shorter pieces, turn up the heat and boil for a couple of minutes before putting in the plums in a single layer. Turn down the heat, cover the pan and simmer the plums for approximately 20 minutes, turning them from time to time. The syrup will become a beautiful clear red. The plums are ready when you can feel that the flesh is soft. Put them, flat side down, in a shallow dish and serve either warm or at room temperature with Crème Pâtissière (see next recipe).

675 g/1 lb 8 oz firm plums

150 g/5 oz/¾ cup caster sugar

425 ml/15 fl oz/2 cups water

Juice of 1 lemon

Cinnamon stick

Menu, *Laconia*, 1929, Cunard.

CUNARD
LINE

# Crème Pâtissière/Custard

600 ml/1 pint/2½ cups long-life full-cream milk

110 g/4 oz/½ cup caster sugar

1 level tablespoon plain flour

1 level tablespoon cornflour

2 large eggs, well beaten

50 g/2 oz/4 tablespoons unsalted butter

Few drops of vanilla extract

I cooked professionally for other people's parties for twenty years and this is the recipe we used for any dish that needed a custard, hot or cold. Commercial custard has its place but this has a particularly delicate flavour that combines perfectly with the Compote. To serve with the Compote of Plums (see opposite), I would suggest flavouring it with vanilla as below. It is also delicious flavoured with almond or even coffee (use almond or coffee essence).

I also suggest using this in the trifle on page 129.

Heat the milk in a pan until just boiling. Take off the heat. Blend the sugar, flour, cornflour and beaten eggs in a bowl, then stir in the hot milk. Wash out the saucepan and return the mixture to the pan. Heat very gently, whisking or stirring continuously. This process will take approximately 10 to 15 minutes and allows the mixture to cook. You will find that the mixture will gradually thicken. Let it just come to the boil and simmer it for 5 minutes still stirring or whisking. Remove from the heat and stir in the butter and vanilla extract.

The custard can be cooled at this point, to wait until you need it. Cover the surface with greaseproof paper to prevent a skin forming (if it does, whisk the custard to disperse it). If you are going to reheat the custard, transfer it to a bowl and wash out the saucepan beforehand. Again, stir the whole time; it catches very easily on the bottom of the pan.

# Devil's Food Cake with Fudge Icing

**Devil's Food Cake was on the Dinner Menu of the *Chusan* on Saturday, 14 January 1961. The other pudding given that day was the sweetly named Coupe Bebé but I haven't been able to track down the recipe. Devil's Food is a fabulous name, too, for this rich dark chocolate cake from America.**

Preheat the oven to 180°C/350°F/Gas Mark 4. The two mixtures are made separately and then blended before cooking. Line a 17.5 cm/7 in. and approximately 7.5 cm/3 in. deep springform cake tin with baking parchment.

For Mixture 1, mix the cocoa and sugar together, then beat in the egg and add the milk. Pour into a small saucepan and cook gently. The mixture catches easily so stir continuously until it has thickened and starts to bubble. Set aside to cool.

For Mixture 2, cream the butter and sugar until pale and fluffy, add the eggs and vanilla extract and beat vigorously. Sift together the flour and the baking powder and fold it into the mixture in stages alternating with the milk until well combined. Stir in Mixture 1 and gently combine it. Pour into the lined tin and bake for approximately 1 hour. The cake is cooked when a skewer inserted into the centre comes out clean.

Leave the cake in the tin for 5 minutes, then turn out on to wire rack to cool. While it is cooling, make the fudge icing.

Melt the butter in a saucepan. Stir in the cocoa and cook gently for a couple of minutes. Take the pan off the heat and stir in the icing sugar and milk. Then beat the mixture with a wooden spoon until it reaches a spreading consistency. This may take up to 10 minutes, but be patient, it will happen. Cut the cake in half and use the icing as a filling and topping. The icing will set after a few hours of chilling. The cake will keep well for several days in a refrigerator.

## For Mixture 1

110 g/4 oz/4 tablespoons cocoa, sieved

150 g/5 oz/¾ cup soft brown sugar

1 large egg

125 ml/4 fl oz/½ cup milk

## For Mixture 2

110 g/4 oz/8 tablespoons butter

175 g/6 oz/¾ cup soft brown sugar

2 large eggs

Few drops of vanilla extract

225 g/8 oz/2 cups plain flour

3 level teaspoons baking powder

125 ml/4 fl oz/½ cup milk

## For the fudge icing

75 g/3 oz/6 tablespoons unsalted butter

50 g/2 oz/2 tablespoons cocoa, sieved

225 g/8 oz/2 cups icing sugar

Small amount of milk to stir in with the icing sugar

# Gooseberry and Ginger Pie

225 g/8 oz/2 cups plain flour

110 g/4 oz/8 tablespoons butter

110 g/4 oz/1 cup icing sugar

Pinch of salt

2 egg yolks

2 tablespoons cold water

450 g/1 lb gooseberries

110 g/4 oz crystallized ginger, chopped into small dice

50 g/2 oz/¼ cup caster sugar

A little milk to brush the top of the pie and a little extra butter to grease the pie plate

I loved the idea of this. It was served for Dinner on 7 August 1968 on the *Queen Elizabeth.* Gooseberries are an underrated fruit. They thrive in the British climate. There are even Gooseberry Clubs in the north of England dedicated to growing the largest gooseberry in the world (58 g/2.06 oz from Marton in Cheshire in 1978). You can make tasty jam from them, combine gooseberry purée with cream and elderflower cordial to make a magical fool or make them into a tart sauce, the perfect accompaniment to grilled mackerel or roast goose. Indeed the *Oxford Companion to Food* considers that this is the reason for their name. They make excellent pies. The sweet pastry, the tart gooseberries and the spicy ginger create a delicious combination of flavours.

You need a shallow dish or ovenproof plate approximately 26 cm/10 in. in diameter.

Process the flour, butter, icing sugar and salt in a food processor until the mixture resembles coarse breadcrumbs. Add the egg yolks and water. Process until the mixture forms a ball. Do not over-process; stop the machine as soon as the ball has formed. Place the pastry in a plastic bag and rest it in the fridge while you 'top and tail' the gooseberries. Butter the pie plate.

Preheat the oven to 180°C/350°F/Gas Mark 4. Divide the pastry into two. Roll out one half to line the plate. Prick the pastry base and fill with the gooseberries and the crystallized ginger. Scatter the caster sugar over the top. Roll out the other half of the pastry to cover the gooseberries. Brush the top with milk and scatter a little sugar on it. Place the dish on a tin baking sheet. This will ensure that the base is firm. Bake for 30 minutes, then cover the pie with foil and bake for a further 10 minutes.

Serve the pie warm rather than hot with cream, crème fraîche or yoghurt.

# Nesselrode Pudding

**This rich frozen pudding was on the Dinner Menu of the *Armadale Castle* on the occasion of the visit of the French fleet in June 1905. Count Nesselrode was a Russian diplomat who lived during the first half of the nineteenth century. Preparation must start well in advance to allow time for freezing.**

Soak the currants and raisins in the rum for at least 15 minutes. Beat the egg yolks with a rotary or electric beater for 1 minute, then add nearly all the sugar. Keep back a couple of tablespoonsful. Keep beating until the mixture is thick and creamy. Heat half the cream in a small saucepan until small bubbles begin to form around the edge of the pan. Very slowly, drop by drop, beat the hot cream into the egg mixture. Return the mixture to the pan and cook over a moderate heat, stirring constantly, until the mixture thickens enough to coat a spoon lightly. Do not let it come near the boil or it will curdle. Remove from the heat and stir in the chestnut purée, vanilla extract, rum, currants and raisins. Chill for about half an hour.

Whip the remaining cream until it thickens slightly, add the rest of the sugar and whip until the cream forms peaks on the beater. Fold into the mixture making sure both are well combined. Brush a 1.2 litre/2 pint mould or mixing bowl with the oil, then fill the mould with the mixture. Cover with cling film and freeze the pudding for 1 hour. Remove from the freezer and beat the crystals into the mixture. Return to the freezer for at least another 5 hours.

Transfer the pudding to the refrigerator about an hour before you want to serve it. To serve, run a knife round the inside of the mould, dip the base briefly in hot water and turn out on to a chilled serving dish. Serve with fresh soft fruit such as raspberries, blue berries and strawberries.

The pudding will keep well in the freezer for a month or so, if you want to prepare it well in advance.

50 g/2 oz/½ cup currants

50 g/2 oz/1½ cup raisins

8 tablespoons dark rum

4 egg yolks

225 g/8 oz/1 cup caster sugar

700 ml/1¼ pints/3 cups double cream

225 g/8 oz tin unsweetened chestnut purée

1 teaspoon vanilla extract

1 teaspoon vegetable oil

Dinner Menu during the visit of the French Fleet, *Armadale Castle*, 1905, Union-Castle.

VISIT OF THE FRENCH FLEET

Royal Naval Review

MENU

DINNER.

HOCK.
Geisenhemer Rothenburg.
1897.

CLARET.
Chat: La Dominique
St. Emilion.
1899.

CHAMPAGNE.
Moët & Chandon's
Dry Imperial.
1898.
Heidsieck & Co.'s
Dry Monopole.
1898.

Hors d'Oeuvres.

Consommé Péluches.
Filletted Soles à l'Imperiale.

Chicken Sauté à la Stanley.
Roast Lamb, Mint Sauce.
French Beans and Potatoes.

Aylesbury Duckling.
Salad.

*Sweets:*
Greengage Tart.
Nesselrode Pudding.
Petit Fours.

Dessert.
Coffee
*(Served on Deck).*

R.M.S. "ARMADALE CASTLE."

*Monday, August 7th, 1905.*

The Union-Castle Mail Steamship Co., Ltd.

DONALD CURRIE & Co., Managers,
3 & 4, Fenchurch St., London, E.C.

# Vanilla Ice Cream

**This is on nearly every menu from the 1920s to the present day. It is an integral part of many shipboard desserts ranging from Peach Melba, served on the original *Queen Mary* in August 1938 (see opposite), to the Baked Alaska served at the Gala Dinner on the *Queen Mary II* on 17 April 2004 on her inaugural transatlantic crossing from Southampton to New York.**

Heat the single cream with the vanilla pod very gently until it just reaches boiling point. Take off the heat. Beat the egg yolks and sugar together until thick, pale and creamy, then whisk in the hot cream. Return the mixture to the saucepan and heat very gently until it thickens. It should just coat the back of a wooden spoon. Do not let it boil. Take off the heat, remove the vanilla pod if you are using one or flavour the custard with the vanilla extract, pour the mixture into a bowl and let it cool completely. When it is cold, whisk the double cream until it stand in peaks and fold it into the cold mixture. Put the bowl into the freezer. After about an hour, take the bowl out of the freezer and whisk, preferably with an electric whisk to break up the ice crystals. Leave in the freezer until it is firm.

450 ml/16 fl oz/2 cups
single cream

1 vanilla pod or a few drops of vanilla extract

3 egg yolks

110 g/4 oz/½ cup caster sugar

150 ml/5 fl oz/½ cup
double cream

# Peach Melba

### For the raspberry sauce

225 g/8 oz raspberries, fresh or frozen

75 g/3 oz/½ cup caster sugar

Juice of 1 lemon

1 peach per person (it must be ripe)

Vanilla ice cream
(see previous recipe)

Peach Melba was invented by Maitre Escoffier, the chef at the newly opened Savoy Hotel in London's Strand in the late nineteenth century. It was inspired by and named after Dame Nellie Melba, the Australian opera star and diva. First served at a dinner party given by the Duc D'Orleans, it consisted of two halves of peach, each topping a ball of ice cream finished off with spun sugar and served in a swan made of ice. Later versions omitted the swan but came to include raspberry purée. Nowadays it can be made at most times of year, but before airfreight it was seasonal according to when fresh peaches and raspberries were available. I found it on a Farewell Dinner Menu, a special occasion on the *Queen Mary*, on Sunday, 7 August 1938.

To make the raspberry sauce, heat the raspberries, sugar and lemon juice gently, stirring continuously, until they come to the boil. Remove from the heat, press through a sieve and leave to cool. Refrigerate until required.

To assemble the peach melbas, first cut a ring round each peach with a knife. Then put them in a deep bowl and cover with boiling water. Leave for 1 minute, then remove from the water and allow to cool. Peel away the skin, slice in half and remove the stone.

Put two balls of ice cream in each bowl. Top each ball with half a peach and pour the raspberry sauce over the top. Serve immediately.

Menu and programme of music, *Araguaya*, 1927, Royal Mail Lines.

# Port and Claret Jelly

Port or Wine Jelly seems to have been quite a favourite during the 1930s. I found it on several menus from this period. Port Wine Jelly was served as the alternative to Soufflé Rothschild (see page 128) at a Farewell Dinner on the *Ausonia* in 1935. Wine Jelly appeared on the Dinner Menu on the *Strathmore* on 27 January 1938. Which one should I feature? I compromised; the recipe below uses both port and claret. It will taste good with any freshly opened light red wine. Don't use a bottle that has been sitting around. If you use a wine with some age, the final taste will be special indeed.

Combine the water, sugar, redcurrant jelly, cinnamon stick, lemon juice and peel in a saucepan large enough to take all ingredients. Bring to the boil. Make a paste with the gelatine and a little of the claret. Add to the mixture and stir gently until you are sure all the gelatine has dissolved. Take off the heat. Then stir in the rest of the claret and the port. Let the mixture cool until lukewarm, then strain it into small glasses to set and chill until required. A spoonful of single cream on the top of the jelly is an added option.

425 ml/15 fl oz/2 cups water

225 g/8 oz/1 cup caster sugar

2 tablespoons redcurrant jelly

Stick of cinnamon

Thinly sliced peel and juice of 2 lemons

25 g/1 oz/1 tablespoon gelatine

425 ml/15 fl oz/2 cups claret

300 ml/10 fl oz/1¼ cups ruby port

Single cream to serve (optional)

# Queen's Pudding

75 g/ 3 oz/1½ cups fresh white breadcrumbs

600 ml/1 pint/scant 3 cups full-cream milk

30 g/1 oz/2 tablespoons butter

Grated zest of 1 lemon

3 eggs, separated

200 g/7 oz/1 cup caster sugar

3 tablespoons raspberry jam

**For the raspberry jam sauce**

3 tablespoons raspberry, strawberry, plum, apricot or blackcurrant jam

2 tablespoons lemon juice (use the juice from the lemon used in the pudding)

3 tablespoons water

**Queen's Pudding or Queen of Puddings is a seventeenth-century milk, breadcrumb and egg pudding. It was given this particular name by the chefs at Buckingham Palace during the reign of Queen Victoria. I found it on a special Silver Jubilee Dinner Menu on the *Windsor Castle* on Wednesday, 14 September 1977.**

Preheat the oven to 180°C/350°F/Gas Mark 4. Butter a 1.25 litre/2 pint/5 cups ovenproof dish. Sprinkle the breadcrumbs in the bottom of the dish. Put the milk, butter and lemon zest into a saucepan and bring slowly to the boil. While it is heating, whisk the egg yolks and 50 g/2 oz/$^1/_4$ cup of the sugar in a bowl until they are pale and thick. Take the milk off the heat, let it cool a little, then whisk into the egg yolks. Strain the custard over the breadcrumbs and leave to soak for 15 minutes. Stand the dish in a roasting tin and fill with water to half way up the side of the dish. Bake in the oven until set. This will take about 25 minutes. Allow to cool slightly.

Turn the oven temperature down to 150°C/300°F/Gas Mark 2. Warm the jam and spread over the top of the pudding. Whisk the egg whites until very stiff, then whisk in the remaining sugar, a little at a time. Pile the meringue mixture on top of the jam. Sprinkle with a little extra caster sugar and bake for a further 15 minutes, until the meringue is crisp and lightly browned.

To make the raspberry jam sauce, heat the jam, lemon juice and water in a small pan. Sieve to make a smooth thin sauce. Test for taste and add more water if preferred.

Serve the pudding hot with the raspberry jam sauce.

# Pouding aux Prunes Anglais/Plum Pudding

We eat this pudding now, almost exclusively, as dessert during traditional Christmas lunch or dinner. However, I found it on a Dinner Menu on the *Saxonia* on 30 August 1961. It was a Gala, so part of another celebration. It is appropriate that *pouding* seems to be a word that the French have taken from the English. Puddings are a dish at which, it is acknowledged, the English have always excelled. This recipe is rich and fruity but not too heavy. It is also suitable for vegetarians. The amount given will fill two medium basins. The puddings will keep for many months. In fact they will taste just as good a year later.

In a large bowl, mix together the raisins, sultanas, currants, candied peel and almonds. Sieve the flour with the mixed spice, cinnamon and nutmeg. Add to the fruit, together with the sugar, breadcrumbs, lemon zest and juice and butter. Mix thoroughly. Beat the eggs with the orange juice and stir into the mixture. Leave to stand overnight. The next day pack into the pudding basins. Leave at least 2.5 cm/1 in. at the top for expansion. Cover with greaseproof paper and foil and tuck each one into a saucepan. Fill the saucepans with water half way up the side of the basins and simmer for 2½ hours.

This recipe is best made ahead of the date you want to use it. On Christmas Day, re-cover with fresh paper and foil and steam for 1 hour before serving.

225g/8 oz/1½ cups raisins

175 g/6 oz/1½ cups sultanas

175 g/6 oz/1½ cups currants

50 g/2 oz/⅓ cup candied peel

25 g/1 oz/¼ cup flaked almonds

25 g/1 oz/¼ cup plain flour

1 teaspoon mixed spice

1 teaspoon cinnamon

½ teaspoon nutmeg

125 g/4 oz/½ cup caster sugar

125 g/4 oz/2 cups fresh white breadcrumbs

Grated zest and juice of 1 lemon

25 g/1 oz/2 tablespoons butter, diced

2 eggs

150 ml/5 fl oz/⅔ cup orange juice

Christmas Day Menu with quotations, *Roslin Castle*, 1897, Union-Castle.

## MENU DU DINER.

"Now let good digestion wait on appetite, and health on both."

Oysters on the half-shell      Olives Farcies

"Dishes alike delightful and appetising."

Consomme Desclignac
Potage a la Prince de Galles

"That's meat and drink to me."

Boiled Turbot and Oyster Sauce
Hatelotes de Sole a la Villeroi

"Slice, I say! slice! that's my humour."

Pluviers a la Perigeuex.
Cotelettes de veau a l'ecarlate
Fillets de Perdre aux a la Princess

"The daintiest that they taste."

Fore-Qtr. of La...
Roast Sirloin Be...
Knuckle of Ve...

"Come you to se...

Turkey in Chains, Wine Sauce
Goose a l'Anglaise
Boiled Fowl and Ox Tongue

Pheasant a la Regence
Hare and Red Currant Jelly

"Dishes that I do love to feed upon."

Prawn Curry

Asparagus      Green Peas
Baked, Boiled, and Saute Potatoes

"Let the sky rain potatoes."

Christmas Plum Pudding
Mince Pies      Champagne Jellies
Darioles d'amandes a la creme
Caramel Pudding      Petit Fours

"Trifles as light as air."

Coffee

## R.M.S. "ROSLIN CASTLE."

CHRISTMAS DAY,
1897.

Commander:
H. DE LA COUR TRAVERS.

# Rhubarb and Apple Charlotte

This has long been a favourite in English country cooking, and has lately become fashionable again since chefs discovered that rhubarb has a tart individual taste particularly delicious combined with other fruits such as apples and oranges. A baked charlotte is a pudding that combines bread and fruit; it is particularly associated with apples, and may have been named after Queen Charlotte, wife of George III, who was said to be a patron of apple growers. This pudding was on the Luncheon Menu of the *Chusan* on Wednesday, 4 January 1961.

675 g/1 lb 8 oz Bramley apples

675 g/1 lb 8 oz rhubarb

Grated zest of 1 lemon

4 tablespoons water

175 g/6 oz/10 tablespoons butter

150 g/6 oz/¾ cup caster sugar

1 thick-sliced white loaf

Preheat the oven to 175°C/350°F/Gas Mark 4. Peel, core and chop the apples into chunks about 2 cm/1 in. square. Chop the rhubarb into the same sized chunks. Put the apple first into a saucepan and add the lemon zest and one tablespoon of the water. Simmer for 10 minutes, then add the rhubarb and the rest of the water. Simmer until the mixture becomes a purée, stirring from time to time. It should take about 25 minutes. Take the pan off the heat and add half the butter, cut into small pieces, and the sugar. Stir until dissolved.

Melt the rest of the butter and use a pastry brush to brush the bread to line the base and sides of a charlotte mould or 18 cm/7 in. cake tin. Cut the crusts off the sliced bread and line the tin base with triangles to fit and slices to fit the sides. Fill the mould with the purée and top with the remainder of the slices of bread. Brush the top with any butter left.

Bake for approximately 40 minutes. The top should be crisp and golden. Allow the Charlotte to cool to lukewarm, then turn it out and serve with custard (see page 115), yoghurt or pouring cream.

# Rice and Raisin Pudding

50 g/2 oz/⅓ cup raisins

2 tablespoons brandy (optional)

50 g/2 oz/4 tablespoons unsalted butter

50 g/2 oz/¼ cup caster sugar

110 g/ 4 oz/½ cup pudding rice

700 ml/1¼ pints/3 cups full-cream milk

300 ml/10 fl oz/1¼ cups single cream

Vanilla pod

Thinly sliced peel of 1 lemon

Fresh nutmeg

**Rice pudding was the only milk pudding I really enjoyed as a child. This is a very grown-up version. For indulgent perfection, serve it with the raspberry sauce in the Peach Melba recipe on page 121 or with fresh soft berries.**

Preheat the oven to 160°C/325°F/Gas Mark 3. Soak the raisins in the brandy while you are preparing the pudding. This part of the recipe is optional; you can stir in the raisins straight from the packet if you prefer.

Melt the butter in a saucepan and dissolve the sugar in it. Add the rice and boil up until the mixture is golden and bubbly. Pour on the milk and cream and heat gently. Split the vanilla pod. Add to the mixture with the lemon peel and stir well until just boiling. Remove from the heat, stir in the raisins (and brandy) and pour into a shallow earthenware dish. Grate some fresh nutmeg over the top. Bake for 2 hours. By this time the mixture should be almost set and there will be a golden skin on the top. Serve warm or at room temperature. It tastes best not too hot and not too cold.

# Soufflé Rothschild

This luxurious pudding was on the First-Class menu of a Farewell Dinner on Cunard's *Ausonia* in 1935. It was originally created by the great chef Antonin Carème, who worked for the millionaire banker, Baron Rothschild, in the nineteenth century, and named the various recipes he invented after his employer. Several recipes I found made it with glacé fruit and on a long voyage this would be necessary, but fresh fruit is even better. The secret of a good soufflé is to mix it gently, cook it in a good, hot oven, resisting the temptation to open the door and peek, and to serve it immediately. On the ship, chefs would have put together baby soufflés, cooked to order in ramekins; you, too, could cook it this way. Feel free to change the fruit that you use as well. It is more important that it should be in perfect condition. I used plums, strawberries and mango (no pineapple available that day) – the result was delicious.

2 ripe peaches

175 g/6 oz strawberries

2 slices fresh pineapple

3 tablespoons Kirsch or Cointreau

3 tablespoons sugar

6 eggs, separated

2 tablespoons whipped cream

Pinch of salt

Icing sugar

Preheat the oven to 200°C/400°F/Gas mark 6. Slice the fruit, retaining the juice. Place in a shallow dish, spoon over the Kirsch or Cointreau and a tablespoon of the sugar. Leave to marinate for at least one hour.

Lightly butter a deep soufflé or charlotte dish, 18 cm/7 in. in diameter. Using a rotary whisk or an electric hand mixer, cream the egg yolks with a tablespoon of the sugar until pale and thickened. Gently stir in the whipped cream together with two tablespoons of juice from the fruit. Whip the egg whites with the salt to a firm consistency and fold very carefully into the mixture, taking care to keep the lightness. Put half the fruit in the bottom of the dish, then half the mixture. Cover with the rest of the fruit and then the rest of the mixture. Stand the dish on a baking tray and bake for approximately 12 minutes. Quickly sprinkle with icing sugar and return to the oven for another 10 minutes so that the sugar caramelizes. Serve straight from the oven.

# Trifle à l'Écossaise

6 trifle sponge cakes

4 tablespoons whisky/sherry

1 small ripe pineapple

160 g/6 oz strawberries

160 g/6 oz raspberries

8 ratafias or small macaroons

300 ml/10 fl oz/1½ cups double cream

25 g/1 oz/¼ cup flaked almonds

This trifle was served at the luncheon after the launch of the *Lusitania* on 7 June 1906. She was launched in Scotland so this is a delicate compliment. I assume that, on that occasion, the liquor used to soak the sponge cakes was whisky. I have also given sherry as an alternative. Trifle is rather like the Dry Martini cocktail (see page 135). No one can agree on the correct recipe. Grown men remember with affection the trifle made by their mothers and grandmothers and come to blows over whether or not jelly and/or jam should be an ingredient. The recipe below has neither jelly nor jam but has given pleasure to a lot of people over many years.

You will need to make up the Crème Pâtissière/Custard as described on page 115. Leave it to cool.

Break up the sponge cakes and use them to fill the bottom of a large glass fruit bowl. Spoon the whisky/sherry over the sponge. Peel and core the pineapple, and cut into chunks. Hull and quarter the strawberries. Scatter the pineapple, strawberries and raspberries over the sponge cakes interspersed with the crumbled macaroons/ratafias.

When the custard is cool, spoon it over the fruit and macaroons. Smooth the top. Whip the cream and spread over the custard. Spread the almonds on a baking tray and toast them until golden. This will only take a minute or two and you need to keep an eye on them so they do not burn. Allow them to cool and scatter on the top of the trifle. Chill until required.

Shakepeare's Touchstone from *As You Like It* laughs on the Union-Castle Menu.

# 6 COCKTAILS AND CANAPÉS

'I must get out of these wet clothes and into a Dry Martini'.

I haven't found out where and when Alexander Woollcott, the New Yorker theatre critic, made this famous remark, but on board a ship it would make perfect sense, after a bracing, and damp turn around the deck.

This is the only section for which I have virtually no factual written reference. There are a few wine lists among the menus I searched but no lists of cocktails. However, pictures and references tell another story. Images of couples enjoying a drink and remarks about parties abound. Passengers were given a Passenger List on arrival. People threw parties for friends who were travelling at the same time and for new acquaintances made during the voyage: social climbers invited celebrities. These festivities were a large part of shipboard life. Inviting the right people, being invited by the right people, meeting in the bar before and after a meal; on all these occasions, the appropriate drink was as important as the company.

Regular passengers forged bonds with barmen and would expect that their exact mix of drink arrived without asking each time they travelled. This is Charles Ryder on the *Queen Mary* in *Brideshead Revisited*: 'The steward returned with whisky and two jugs, one of iced water, the other of boiling water; I mixed them to the right temperature. He watched and said: "I'll remember that's how you take it, sir." Most passengers had fads, he was paid to fortify their self-esteem.'

The 1920s and 1930s were the cocktail years. Bear in mind that the 1920s were the years of prohibition in the United States. The ships offered the possibility of a drink, which you couldn't get at home. French Line for instance, specially slanted their advertisements to appeal to drinkers. There are many tales of stewards having to put their inebriated customers to bed on the trip across from New York to Europe.

The recipes I have chosen are all classics from this period or earlier. Several were invented by the legendary barman, Harry MacElhone (spellings of his name vary), who first worked at Ciro's in London and went on to found Harry's Bar at 5 rue Daunou, Paris. The widow of his son, Andy, still runs that bar. There's a Harry's Bar in Venice, which is still flourishing too. The Bellini, a delicious mixture of champagne and fresh white peach juice was invented there in 1948 and named after Giovanni Bellini, one of the great artists of Venice.

Post war, barmen were still creating new cocktails on the ships. Sally Spooner remembers: 'On the *Orsova*, the barman had invented a gin based cocktail full of fruit, cucumber and mint. He called it "The Choirmaster". Us girls, too young for the gin, had "Choirboys", the fruit etc. without the alcohol'.

For those who want to party, I have included two recipes for Rum Punch; hot for winter, iced for summer.

Also in this section there are a couple of recipes for canapés. These come from menus where they were served at dinner as a savoury at the end of the meal. They are mostly served warm (not too hot or people will drop them). They do make delicious light eats to stave off hunger while sampling one of the cocktail recipes or with any other aperitif of your choice.

Most of the recipes that you find here have a different measuring system. It is based on percentage part of each cocktail. I give below the quantities of a standard barman's measure, but if you haven't got one you can always use a shot glass or even an egg cup. A standard barman's measure is 25 ml, which is just over 1 fl oz. A double is 50 ml or 2 fl oz.

Opposite and right: By the pool or in the bar, sipping a cocktail was a delightful way to pass the time.

# Bronx Cocktail

The Bronx was invented about a hundred years ago at the Big Brass Rail, a bar in the Waldorf Astoria, New York. The bar was demolished and the Empire State Building now stands in its place.

Combine all the ingredients except the orange slice in the shaker. Shake well. Strain into a cocktail glass/es or a small tumbler/s. Garnish with the orange slice.

2 parts London gin

1 part sweet vermouth

1 part dry vermouth

2 parts freshly squeezed orange juice

Dash of Angostura Bitters

Cocktail shaker half full of ice

Orange slice to garnish

# Champagne Cocktail

Champagne Cocktail is a celebration drink for special birthdays, to toast the bride and groom and to wet the baby's head at his or her christening. Or you could just drink it to celebrate the pleasure of being alive.

Put the lump of sugar in a champagne flute. Shake the Bitters over the sugar and add the cognac. Top up with very cold non-vintage champagne or sparkling wine.

1 small lump of sugar

3 dashes of Angostura Bitters

½ measure of cognac

Very cold non-vintage champagne or 'méthode champenoise' sparkling wine

Left and opposite: Celebration menus from Cunard and P&O.

# Manhattan Cocktail

2 parts Bourbon whiskey

1 part dry vermouth

1 part sweet vermouth

Dash of Angostura Bitters

Jug of ice

Maraschino cherry to serve

The Manhattan was invented in New York around 1890. It became a great favourite and crossed the Atlantic sometime during the years that followed. I like to think this was the result of it being on the list of cocktails in one of the bars of the great liners, perhaps the *Lusitania* or her sister-ship, the *Aquitania*. By 1906, it was well enough known in England to appear in the latest edition of Mrs Beeton's *The Book of Household Management*. Don't forget the maraschino cherry!

Pour the whiskey, vermouths and Angostura Bitters into the jug of ice. Stir and strain into a stemmed glass. Serve with a cocktail cherry on a stick in each glass.

# Sidecar

2 parts brandy

1 part Cointreau

Juice of half a lemon

Cocktail shaker half full of ice cubes

The Sidecar was invented by Harry MacElhone at Harry's Bar. He dedicated the drink to a captain (whether naval or military is not known) who, it is said, drove into the bar on a motorcycle with sidecar.

Add all the ingredients to the ice in the shaker. Shake for 6 to 8 seconds and strain into a cocktail glass.

# Rum Punch

This is not strictly a cocktail but I include a recipe for both a hot and a cold one. Somehow it seems appropriate for ships. Perhaps it is the association of rum with the 'tot' doled out each day in the Royal Navy as part of a sailor's perks. Punch is essentially a drink for company so quantities are given for a group. The recipes are adapted from the 1880 edition of Mrs Beeton's *The Book of Household Management*. I can't do better than quote from Mrs Beeton herself on how many people these will serve. 'Allow a quart for 4 persons; but this information must be taken *in grano salis*, for the capacities of persons for this kind of beverage are generally supposed to vary considerably.'

To make the Hot Rum Punch, rub the sugar lumps over one of the lemons to absorb the oil from the skin. Put the sugar in a large heatproof bowl. Juice one of the lemons and add to the bowl. Pour over the boiling water and stir to dissolve the sugar. Add the rum, brandy and nutmeg. Slice the second lemon and add to the mixture. Mix well and use a ladle to serve immediately while it is still hot.

To make the Chilled Rum Punch, peel the lemon into thin strips and put these in a large bowl with the sugar and water. Stir to dissolve the sugar, then add the rum, curacao and wine. Squeeze the juice from the lemon and add to the punch. Add cracked ice to the bowl, give it a stir and serve each glass with some ice in it.

### For the Hot Rum Punch

110 g/4 oz/1 cup sugar lumps

2 lemons (use unwaxed if possible)

300 ml/10 fl oz dark rum

300 ml/10 fl oz brandy

½ teaspoon grated nutmeg

600 ml/1 pint boiling water

### For the Chilled Rum Punch

1 large lemon (unwaxed if possible)

110 g/4 oz/1 cup icing sugar

700 ml/1¼ pints sparkling water

1 bottle of rum

2 small glasses Curacao

1 bottle of champagne or sparkling wine

Ice

# Dry Martini

1 part dry vermouth,

6 parts gin

A ²/₃ pint jug of ice

Lemon peel

The Dry Martini was invented in the Knickerbocker Hotel, New York, in about 1910. The bartender who gave the cocktail its name was Signor Martini. The vermouth originally used was Noilly Prat.

Should I even give a recipe for a Dry Martini? Good men have come to blows over the proportion of gin to vermouth. It goes without question that it must be the best London gin – Booths or Gordons. The general agreement is also that the spirits must be poured over ice, before being strained into a martini glass. But how much ice and how much stirring? James Bond caused consternation when he asked for his martini 'shaken not stirred', so my recipe goes for stirring. I like the addition of a tiny strip of lemon peel but leave it out if you are a real purist.

Pour the vermouth and gin into the jug. Give the mixture a good stir. Strain the liquid into chilled, stemmed glasses and garnish each with a twist of thin lemon peel.

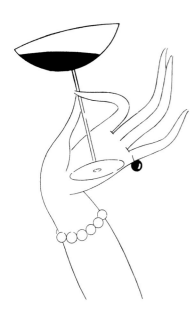

# White Lady

3 parts gin

2 parts Cointreau

2 parts freshly squeezed lemon juice

Ice

The White Lady was invented at Ciro's Club in London by Harry MacElhone in honour of a mysterious white lady.

Half fill a cocktail shaker with ice and add all of the other ingredients. Shake for 10 seconds and strain into a stemmed glass.

# Beurek à la Turque

These delicious little morsels were served as a savoury at the end of dinner on the *Laconia* on a West Indian Cruise on Saturday, 23 February 1929. I think there must have been a Turk working in the galley since they originate from Turkey and I never found them on any other menu. They are more usually spelt 'Borek' and can be stuffed with a variety of different cheese or meat fillings. I have listed one of each. They can be made ahead of time since they will reheat easily. They are perfect eaten warm with one of the cocktail recipes or to accompany a glass of cold white wine. I give the filling recipes first since you will need to make these before you start the Beureks. You also need a pastry brush to work with filo pastry.

While the filo pastry is defrosting, make the fillings as follows: For the cheese and spinach filling, wash the spinach well, shred and place in a saucepan with the butter. Cook gently for a few minutes. Allow it to cool. Crumble the feta cheese and mix well with the spinach and the herbs. Season with the pepper. Feta is very salty so you will probably not need to salt the mixture.

For the meat filling, peel and chop the onion very finely. Heat the oil in a shallow pan and fry the onion until soft. Add the lamb and fry gently until it changes colour. Add the pine nuts and fry for 2 minutes. Season with cinnamon, salt and pepper. Add the water and simmer for a few more minutes until the water is absorbed and the meat mixture is soft.

Preheat the oven to 200°C/400°F/Gas Mark 6.

To make the Meat Beureks, melt the butter in a small saucepan. Filo has to be used reasonably quickly, otherwise it will dry out and crack, so it is best to remove one or two sheets from the packet at a time. Cut each sheet into four rectangular strips. Brush each strip with melted butter. Put a teaspoon of meat filling at one end and fold the filo over it making a triangle. Continue down the strip over and over again until the whole strip

450 g/1 lb pack of frozen filo pastry (from the freezer cabinet of the supermarket)

225 g/8 oz/8 tablespoons butter

**For the cheese and spinach filling**

225 g/8 oz spinach

15 g/1 oz/1 tablespoon butter

225 g/8 oz/1¼ cups feta cheese

1 tablespoon green herbs, any mixture of parsley, mint, oregano is good, or alternatively use parsley alone

Black pepper to taste

**For the meat filling**

1 small onion

2 tablespoons olive oil

225 g/8 oz/1 cup finely minced lamb

2 tablespoons pine nuts

1 level teaspoon cinnamon

Salt and pepper to taste

About 3 tablespoons of water

is folded. Brush the top of the triangle with melted butter and bake on a baking tray lined with baking parchment until crisp and golden.

Triangles are traditional for Meat Beureks. Cheese and Spinach Beureks are rolled into a tube shape. Cut the strips as above and brush with melted butter. Lay a teaspoon of filling at one end. Fold the nearest short edge over it, then fold the two longer edges in a little to stop the mixture leaking out. Roll up and brush with melted butter and bake as above.

Celebration menu, *Iberia*, c. 1954, P&O.

# Beignets de Fromage

The *Lancastria* made her landfall on Friday 4 October 1935. The menu for the night before was entirely in French including the title, Diner D'Adieu. The savoury listed was these crisp, piquant cheese pastries made from choux pastry. In 1935 they would have been deep-fried. However, they are just as good and much less trouble for the cook baked in a hot oven, so that is what I have suggested. Either way, they make delicious bite-size morsels to serve with drinks.

Preheat the oven to 230°C/450°F/Gas Mark 8. Sift the flour with the mustard powder, cayenne pepper and salt. Melt the butter in the water and bring to the boil. Take the pan off the heat and immediately tip in all the flour mixture. Beat with a wooden spoon until the paste leaves the sides of the pan. Transfer to a food processor and allow to cool for 10 minutes. Switch on and add the eggs one by one through the feed tube, processing between each addition until the mixture is smooth. Retain a quarter or so of the cheese and add the rest to the mixture. Process to mix it in.

Line a baking tray with silicone paper. Using two teaspoons drop spoonsful of the mixture on to the sheet. Brush with the glaze and top each beignet with a little grated parmesan. Bake for 10 minutes, then reduce the heat to 180°C/350°F/Gas Mark 4 and continue cooking for a further 20 to 30 minutes. The beignets are ready when they are golden brown. Either serve immediately or cool on a wire tray and reheat gently when required.

Beignets will freeze well. Simply reheat from frozen in a moderate oven to serve.

They are also delicious stuffed with creamed salmon or a cheese sauce.

150 g/5 oz/1½ cups plain flour

1 dessertspoon mustard powder

¼ teaspoon cayenne pepper

¼ teaspoon salt

300 ml/10 fl oz/1½ cups water

110 g/4 oz/8 tablespoons butter

3 large eggs

110 g/4 oz/¾ cup grated fresh parmesan cheese

1 egg yolk mixed with a little milk to glaze

Diner D'Adieu, *Araguaya*, 1927, Royal Mail Lines.

Diner D'Adieu

# BIBLIOGRAPHY

Bainbridge, B. *Every Man for Himself* Abacus, London, 1999

Beck, S., Bertholle, L. and Child, J. *Mastering the Art of French Cooking* Cassell, London, 1971

Beeton, I. *The Book of Household Management* Ward, Lock & Co., London, 1888

Campbell, S. and Conran, C. *Poor Cook* Sphere Books, London, 1972

*Cookery Year Readers Digest, The* London, 1974

Coons, L. and Varias Palgrave, A. *Tourist Third Cabin: Steamship Travel in the Interwar Years* MacMillan, Basingstoke, 2003

*Cordon Bleu Desserts and Puddings* Penguin, London, 1975

Davidson, A. *The Oxford Companion to Food* Oxford University Press, Oxford, 1999

Edington, S. *National Trust Recipes*, The National Trust, London, 1996

Farmer, F. M. *The Boston Cooking School Book* McClelland & Stewart, Toronto

Fitzgibbon, T. *A Taste of Scotland* Jarrold & Sons, Norwich, 1970

Forster, E.M. *A Passage to India* Penguin, London, 1970

Foucart, B., Offrey, C., Robichon, F., and Villers, C. *Normandie: Queen of the Seas* The Vendome Press, New York, 1985

Gregory, A. *The Golden Age of Travel* Cassell, London, 1991

Hazan, M. *The Classic Italian Cookbook* MacMillan, London, 1980

Hopkinson, S. and Bareham, L. *The Prawn Cocktail Years* MacMillan, London, 1997

Hutchings, D. F. *Pride of the North Atlantic* Waterfront, Settle, Yorkshire, 2003

*Larousse Gastronomique* Mandarin, London, 1990

McMillan, B. and Lehrer, S. *Titanic: Fortune and Fate* Simon & Schuster, New York, 1998

Miller, B. *Ocean Liners* Magna Books, Leicester, 1990

Morris, S. *Cardamom & Coriander* Metro Books, London, 1998

Olney, R. *Simple French Food* Penguin Books, London, 1974

*Oxford Hachette French Dictionary, The* Oxford University Press, Oxford, 1994

Padfield, P. *Beneath the House Flag of the P&O* Hutchison & Co., London, 1981

Paston-Williams, S. *Traditional Puddings* The National Trust, London, 2002

Roden, C. *A Book of Middle Eastern Food* Penguin, London, 1980

Saulnier, L. *Le Repertoire de la Cuisine* Leon Jaeggi & Sons Ltd, Staines.

Smith, M. *Fine English Cookery* Faber Paperbacks, Whitstable, Kent, 1983

Smith, M. *Grace and Flavour à la Mode* BBC, London, 1980

Spry, C. *The Constance Spry Cookbook* Pan Books, London, 1972

Steele, J. *Queen Mary* Phaidon Press Ltd, London, 1995

Wall, R. *Ocean Liners* Collins, London, 1978

Waugh, E. *Brideshead Revisited* first published 1945, reissued by Penguin, London 2003

WI, The and Smith, M. *A Cook's Tour of Britain* WI Books, London, 1984

Willan, A. *Readers Digest Complete Guide to Cookery* Dorling Kindersley, London, 1989

# PICTURE CREDITS

Unless otherwise stated, illustrations are copyright
© National Maritime Museum, London.
Reproduction numbers for these are listed below.

We are grateful to the following for their kind
permission to reproduce many of the menus that
appear in this book, in the collection of the Museum:
Anchor Line, Cunard; Elder Dempster; Peninsular
and Oriental Steam Navigation Company (P&O
Archive); Royal Mail; Union-Castle Line; Waterline
and the following archives:

*Page 12* Bridgeman Art Library; *16* © Cunard
(courtesy Open Agency); *18* P&O Archive; *35* © Bill
Miller Collection; *20, 42, 43* Private Collection,
courtesy the author; *85* Matson Line (Private
Collection, courtesy the author)

The front cover illustration reproduces details of
'The Empress of Britain', Canadian Pacific Railway
poster, 1931–40 (© V&A Images) and 'A contrast in
train accommodation of 1830/1930' by A. R.
Thompson (National Railway Museum/ Science &
Society Picture Library)

NMM
*Page 1* F3584; *2* G10892; *6* F3605; *9* D2277; *10*
P82038; *15* A2988, A2989; *19* detail from F3589; *22*
P84530; *25* P82350; *26* P85862; *27* D2277; *28*
P89606; *30* F3581; *33* P82888; *37* P82887; *38* F3594;
*41* F3584; *45* F3583; *47* F3596, F3856; *49* detail
from G13322; *52* F3607; *59* F3608; *60* F3667; *62*
P82935; *63* F3593; *64* F5610; *66* detail from F3856;
*69* P91296; *71* P82053; *73* F3859-1; *75* F3598; *81*
F3604; *88* F3580; *93* P82110; *95* D9696; *97* F3611,
F3612; *99* detail from G10892; *103* F3593; *109*
F3600, F3602; *111* F3670; *114* F3593-2; *119* F3592;
*121* F3854; *125* F3588, F3587; *129* F3669; *130*
P82545; *131* P84520; *132* F3595; *133* F3855; *137*
F3858, F3857; *139* F3585

*Page 3* detail of 'A contrast in train accommodation
of 1830/1930' by A. R. Thompson (National Railway
Museum/Science & Society Picture Library)

# INDEX